ULTIMATE X-MEN

RETURN TO WEAPON X

WRITER
MARK MILLAR

PENCILS
ADAM KUBERT
W/ TOM RANEY
& TOM DERENICK

INKS
ART THIBERT
W/ SCOTT HANNA,
JOE KUBERT,
DANNY MIKI
& LARY STUCKER

COLORS
TRANSPARENCY
DIGITAL
W/ RICHARD ISANOVE
& DAVID STEWART

LETTERS
RICHARD
STARKINGS
& COMICRAFT'S
WES'N'SAIDA!

ASSISTANT EDITOR
PETE FRANCO

EDITOR
MARK POWERS

EDITOR IN CHIEF
JOE QUESADA

PRESIDENT
BILL JEMAS

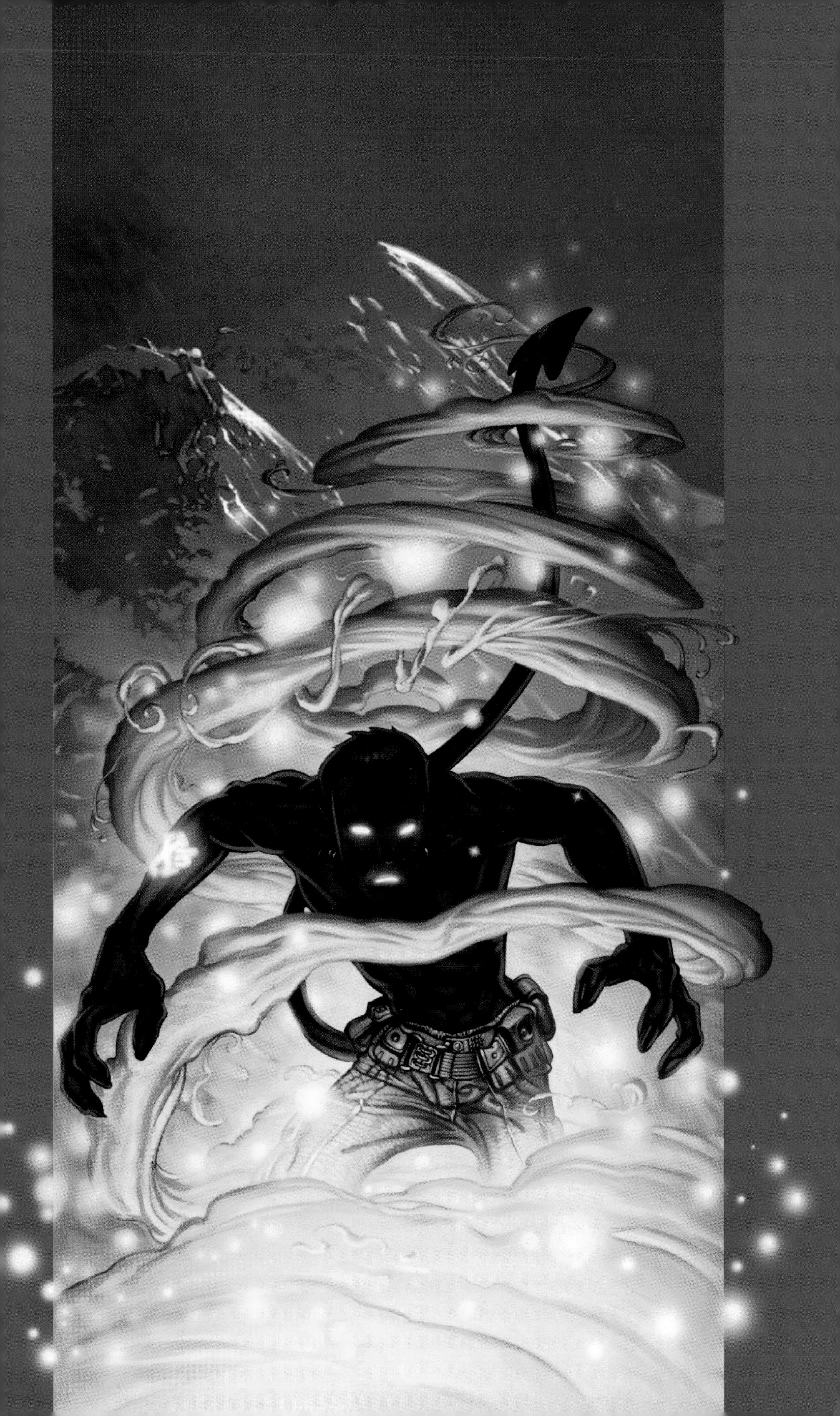

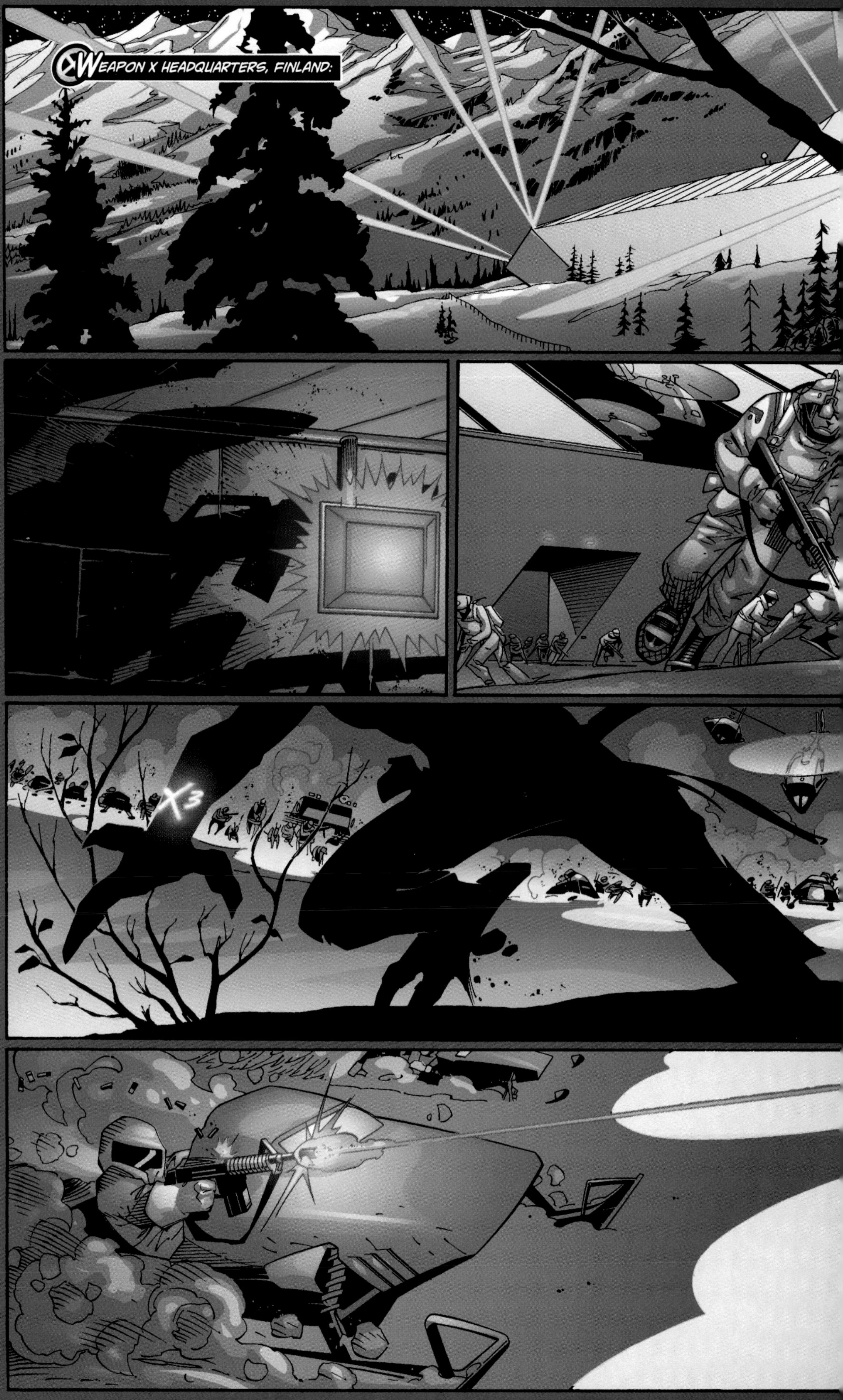
WEAPON X HEADQUARTERS, FINLAND:
X3

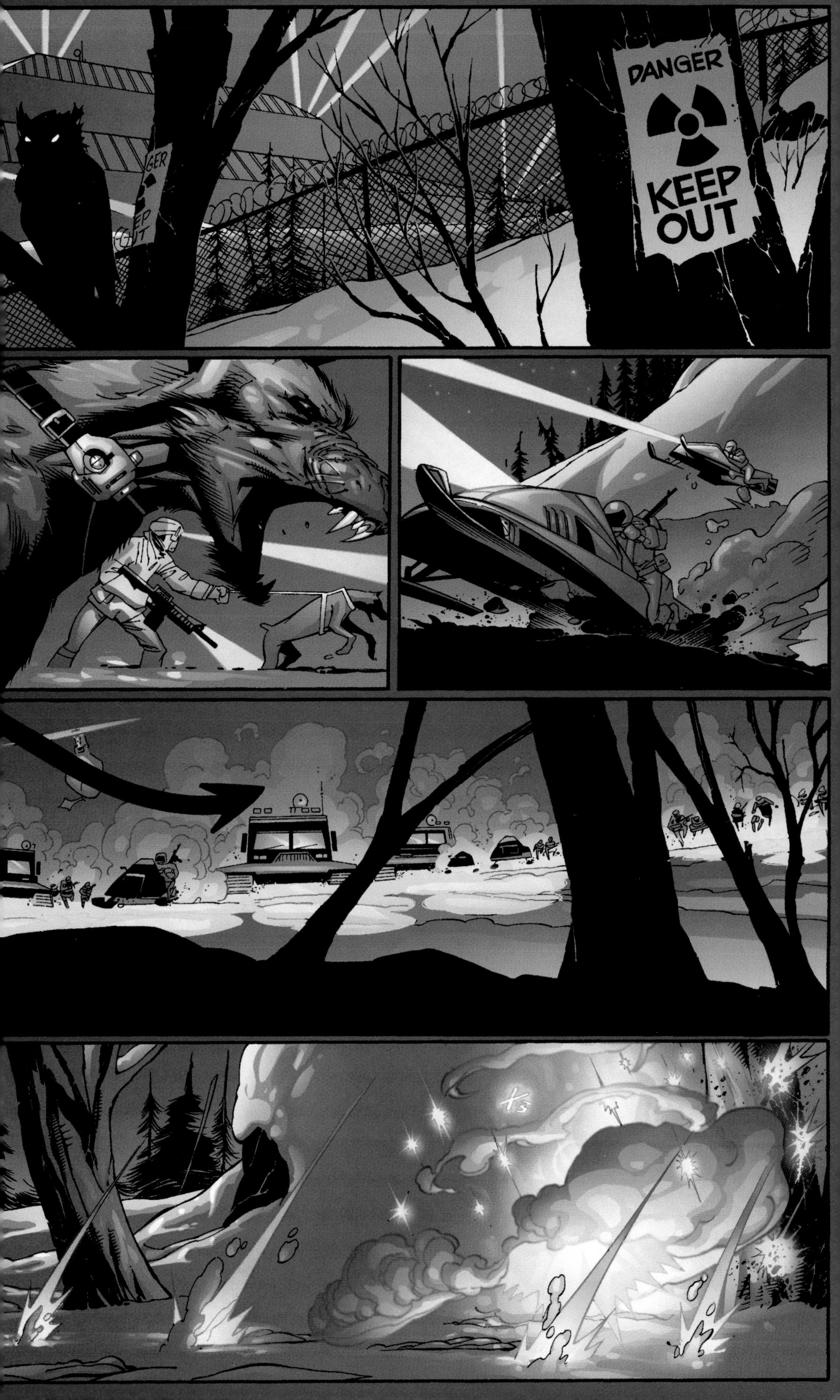
DANGER
KEEP OUT

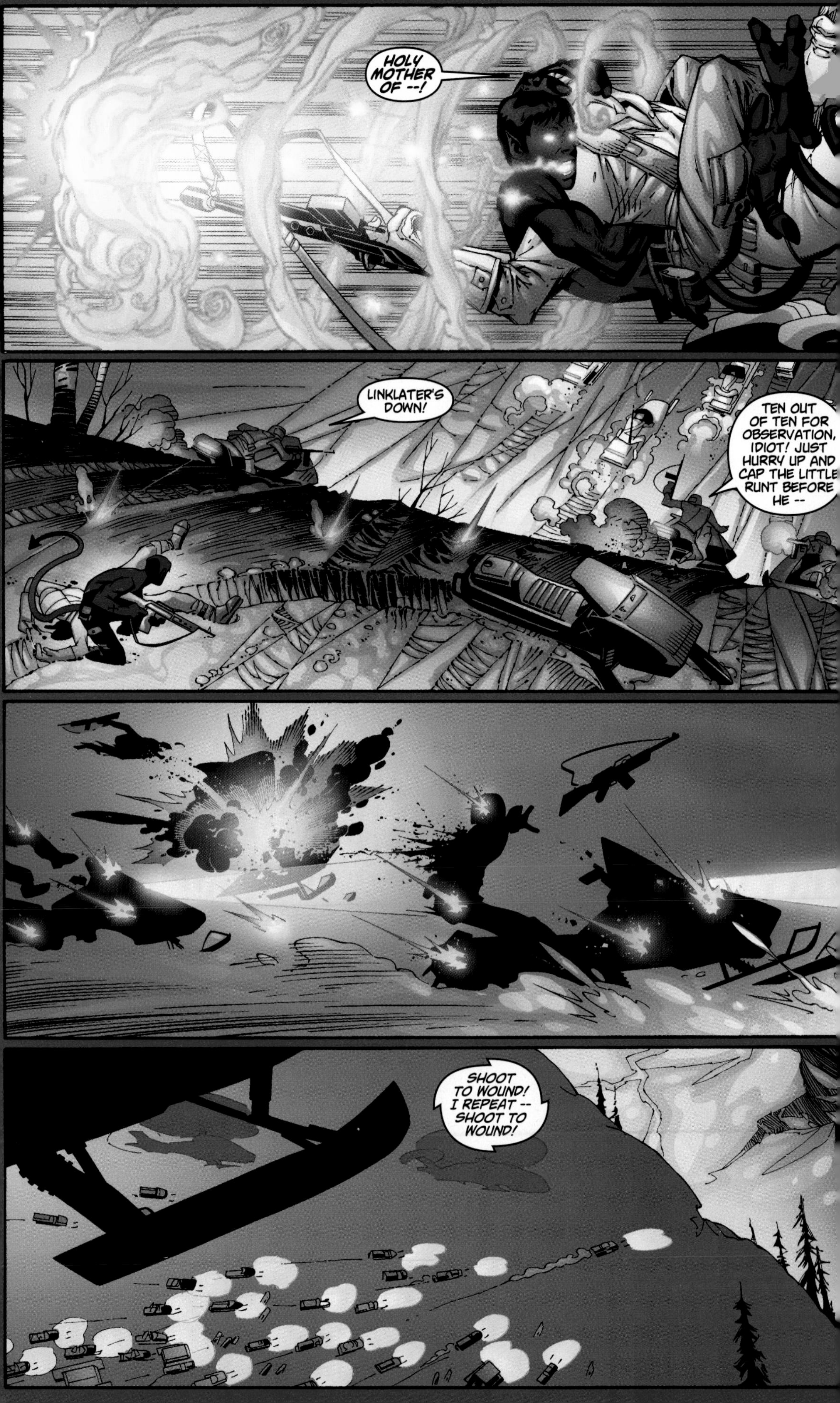
HOLY MOTHER OF --!
LINKLATER'S DOWN!
TEN OUT OF TEN FOR OBSERVATION, IDIOT! JUST HURRY UP AND CAP THE LITTLE RUNT BEFORE HE --
SHOOT TO WOUND! I REPEAT -- SHOOT TO WOUND!

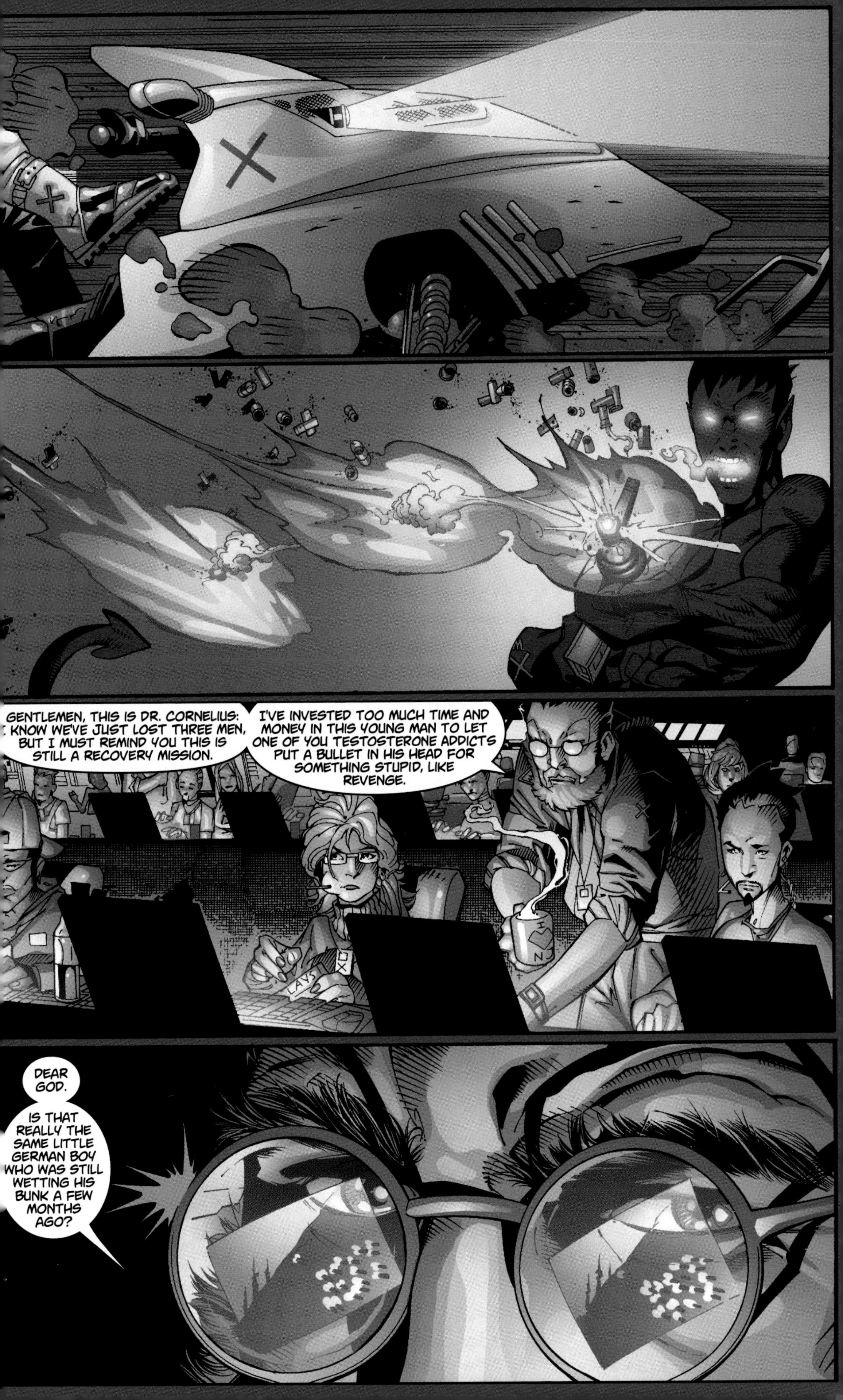
GENTLEMEN, THIS IS DR. CORNELIUS: I KNOW WE'VE JUST LOST THREE MEN, BUT I MUST REMIND YOU THIS IS STILL A RECOVERY MISSION.
I'VE INVESTED TOO MUCH TIME AND MONEY IN THIS YOUNG MAN TO LET ONE OF YOU TESTOSTERONE ADDICTS PUT A BULLET IN HIS HEAD FOR SOMETHING STUPID, LIKE REVENGE.
LAYS
DEAR GOD.
IS THAT REALLY THE SAME LITTLE GERMAN BOY WHO WAS STILL WETTING HIS BUNK A FEW MONTHS AGO?

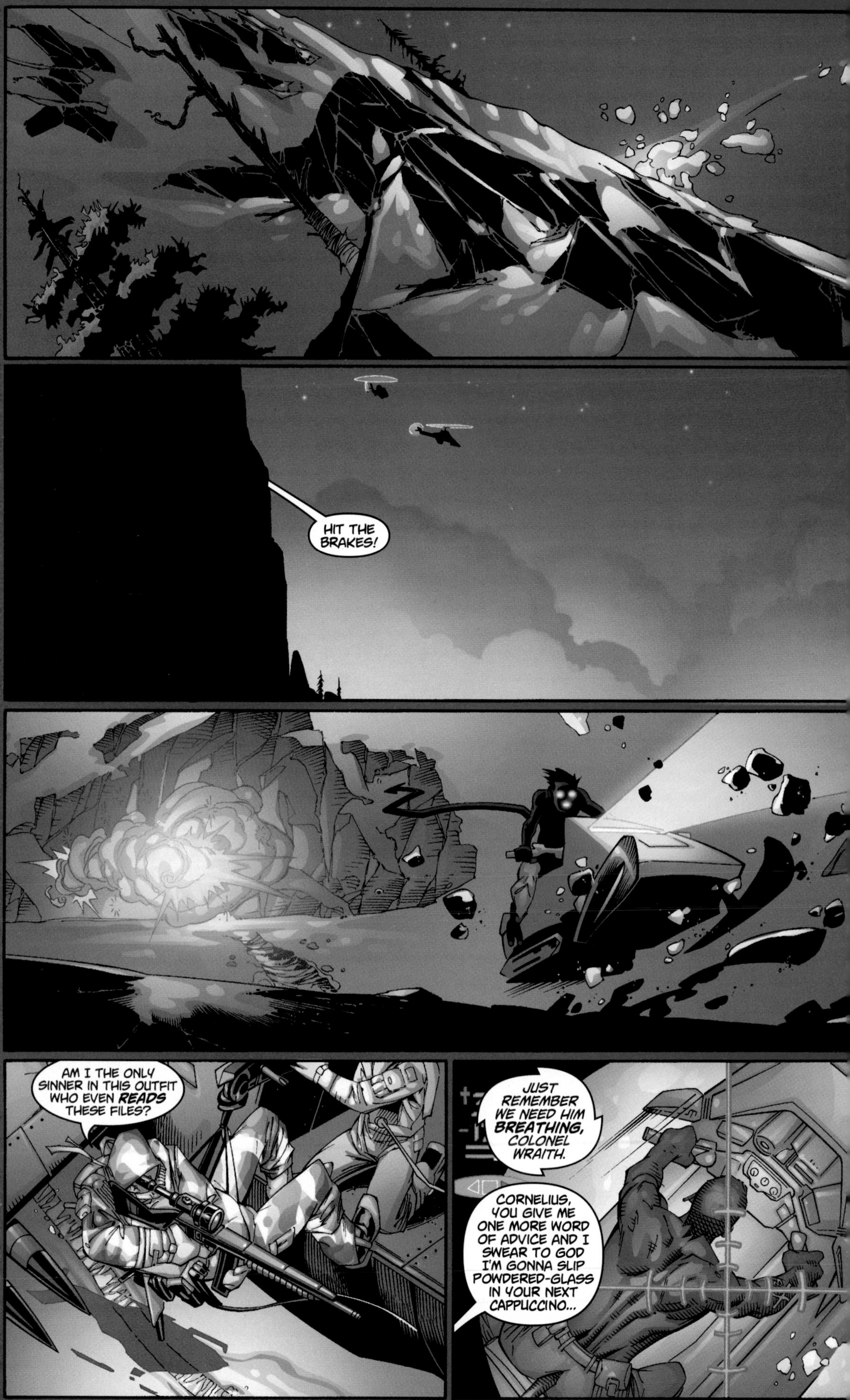
HIT THE BRAKES!
AM I THE ONLY SINNER IN THIS OUTFIT WHO EVEN READS THESE FILES?
JUST REMEMBER WE NEED HIM BREATHING, COLONEL WRAITH.
CORNELIUS, YOU GIVE ME ONE MORE WORD OF ADVICE AND I SWEAR TO GOD I'M GONNA SLIP POWDERED-GLASS IN YOUR NEXT CAPPUCCINO...

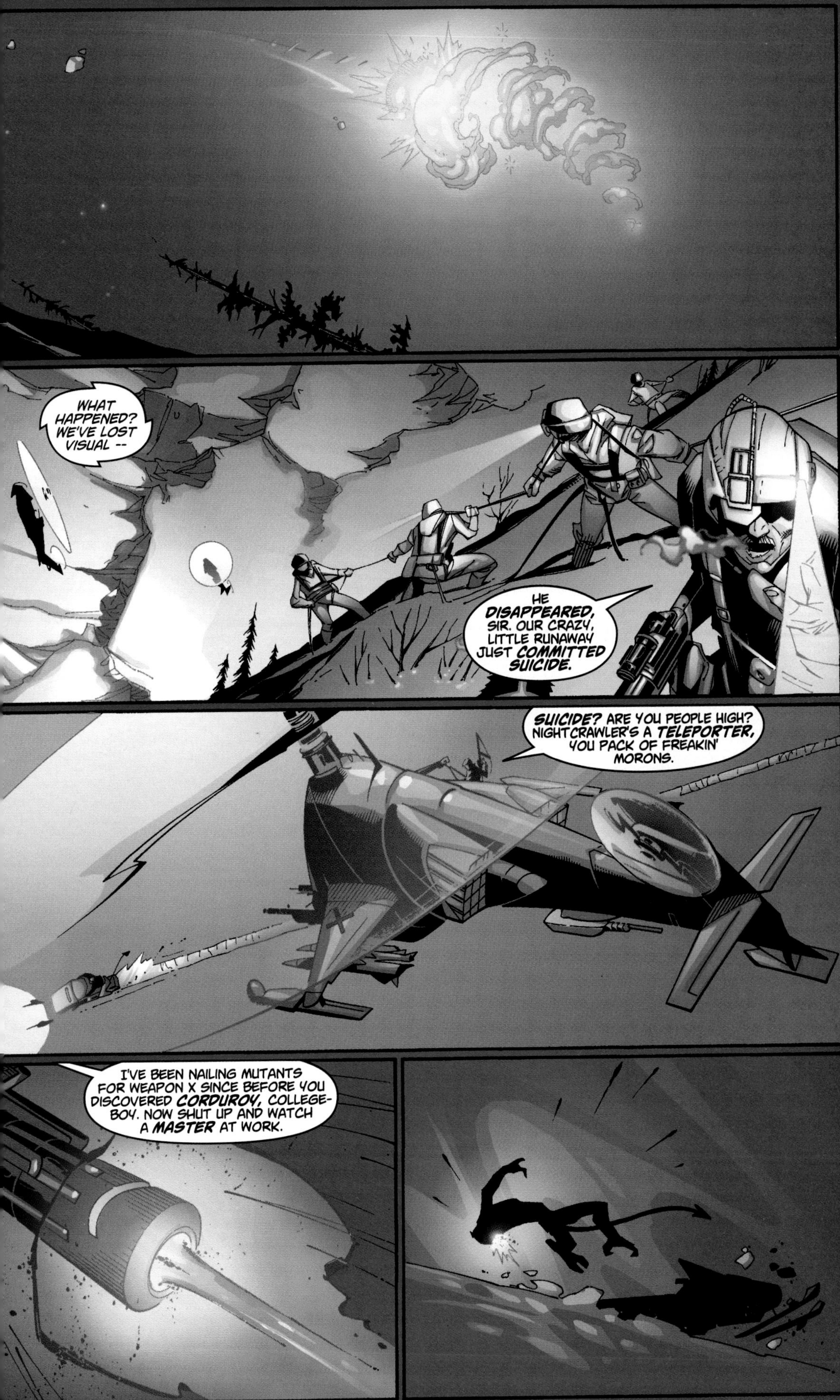
WHAT HAPPENED? WE'VE LOST VISUAL --
HE DISAPPEARED, SIR. OUR CRAZY, LITTLE RUNAWAY JUST COMMITTED SUICIDE.
SUICIDE? ARE YOU PEOPLE HIGH? NIGHTCRAWLER'S A TELEPORTER, YOU PACK OF FREAKIN' MORONS.
I'VE BEEN NAILING MUTANTS FOR WEAPON X SINCE BEFORE YOU DISCOVERED CORDUROY, COLLEGE-BOY. NOW SHUT UP AND WATCH A MASTER AT WORK.

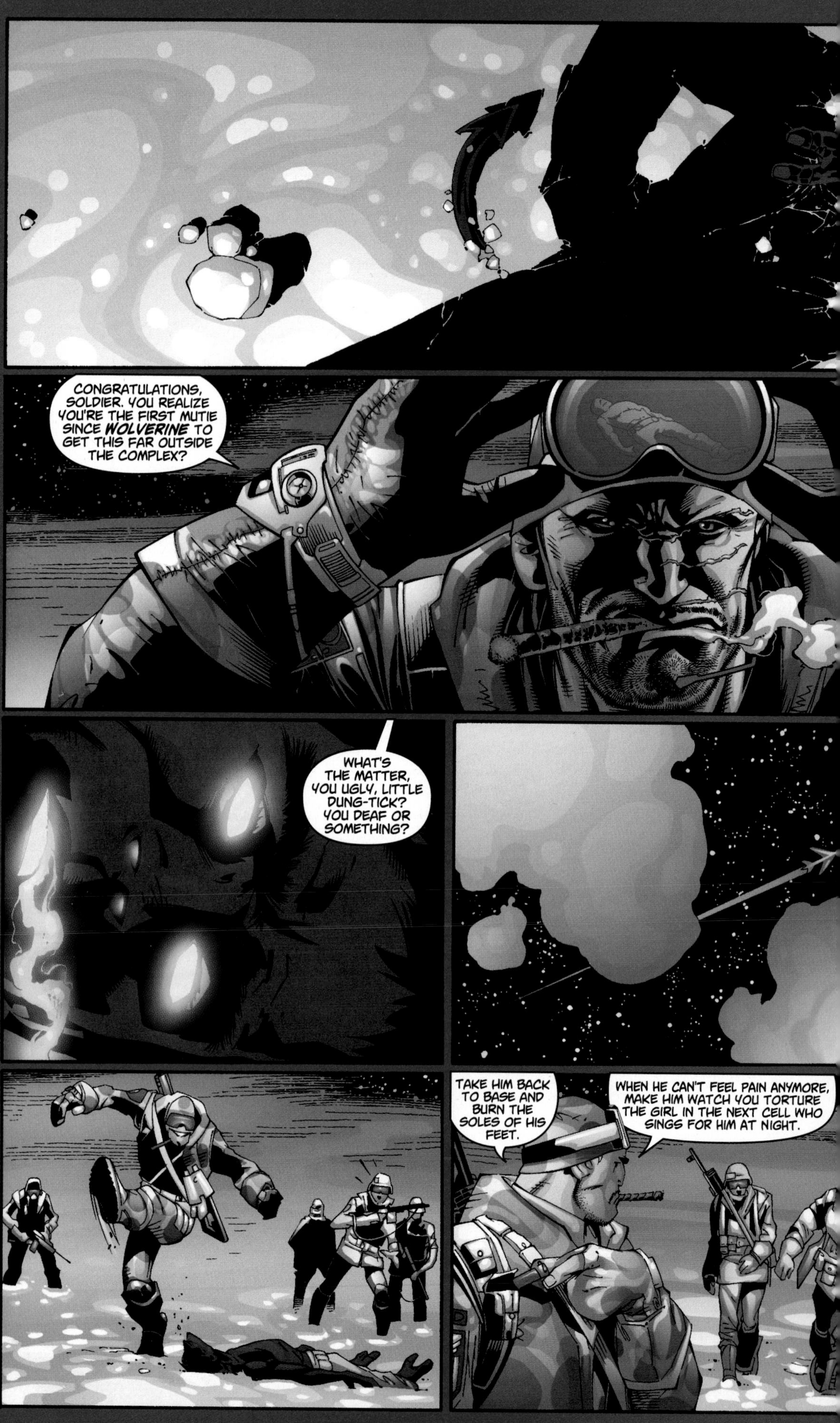
CONGRATULATIONS, SOLDIER. YOU REALIZE YOU'RE THE FIRST MUTIE SINCE WOLVERINE TO GET THIS FAR OUTSIDE THE COMPLEX?
WHAT'S THE MATTER, YOU UGLY, LITTLE DUNG-TICK? YOU DEAF OR SOMETHING?
TAKE HIM BACK TO BASE AND BURN THE SOLES OF HIS FEET.
WHEN HE CAN'T FEEL PAIN ANYMORE, MAKE HIM WATCH YOU TORTURE THE GIRL IN THE NEXT CELL WHO SINGS FOR HIM AT NIGHT.

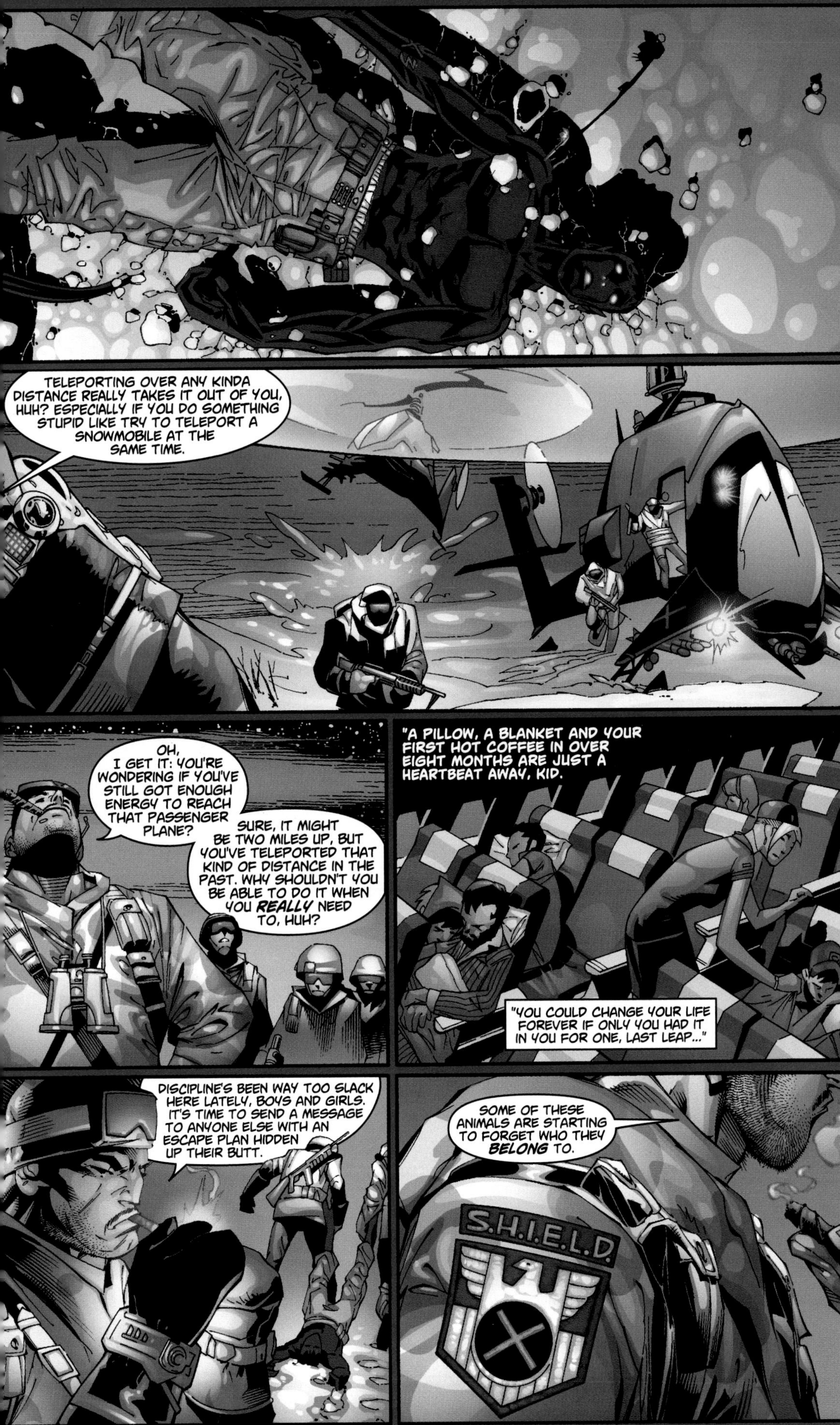
TELEPORTING OVER ANY KINDA DISTANCE REALLY TAKES IT OUT OF YOU, HUH? ESPECIALLY IF YOU DO SOMETHING STUPID LIKE TRY TO TELEPORT A SNOWMOBILE AT THE SAME TIME.
OH, I GET IT: YOU'RE WONDERING IF YOU'VE STILL GOT ENOUGH ENERGY TO REACH THAT PASSENGER PLANE?
SURE, IT MIGHT BE TWO MILES UP, BUT YOU'VE TELEPORTED THAT KIND OF DISTANCE IN THE PAST. WHY SHOULDN'T YOU BE ABLE TO DO IT WHEN YOU *REALLY* NEED TO, HUH?
"A PILLOW, A BLANKET AND YOUR FIRST HOT COFFEE IN OVER EIGHT MONTHS ARE JUST A HEARTBEAT AWAY, KID.
"YOU COULD CHANGE YOUR LIFE FOREVER IF ONLY YOU HAD IT IN YOU FOR ONE, LAST LEAP..."
DISCIPLINE'S BEEN WAY TOO SLACK HERE LATELY, BOYS AND GIRLS. IT'S TIME TO SEND A MESSAGE TO ANYONE ELSE WITH AN ESCAPE PLAN HIDDEN UP THEIR BUTT.
SOME OF THESE ANIMALS ARE STARTING TO FORGET WHO THEY *BELONG* TO.
S.H.I.E.L.D.

MARK MILLAR
writer

ADAM KUBERT
pencils

ART THIBERT
inks

RICHARD ISANOVE
colors

RICHARD STARKINGS
& COMICRAFT'S
WES ABBOTT
letters

PETE FRANCO
assistant editor

MARK POWERS
editor

JOE QUESADA
editor in chief

BILL JEMAS
president

RETURN TO
WEAPON X

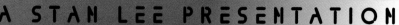

A STAN LEE PRESENTATION

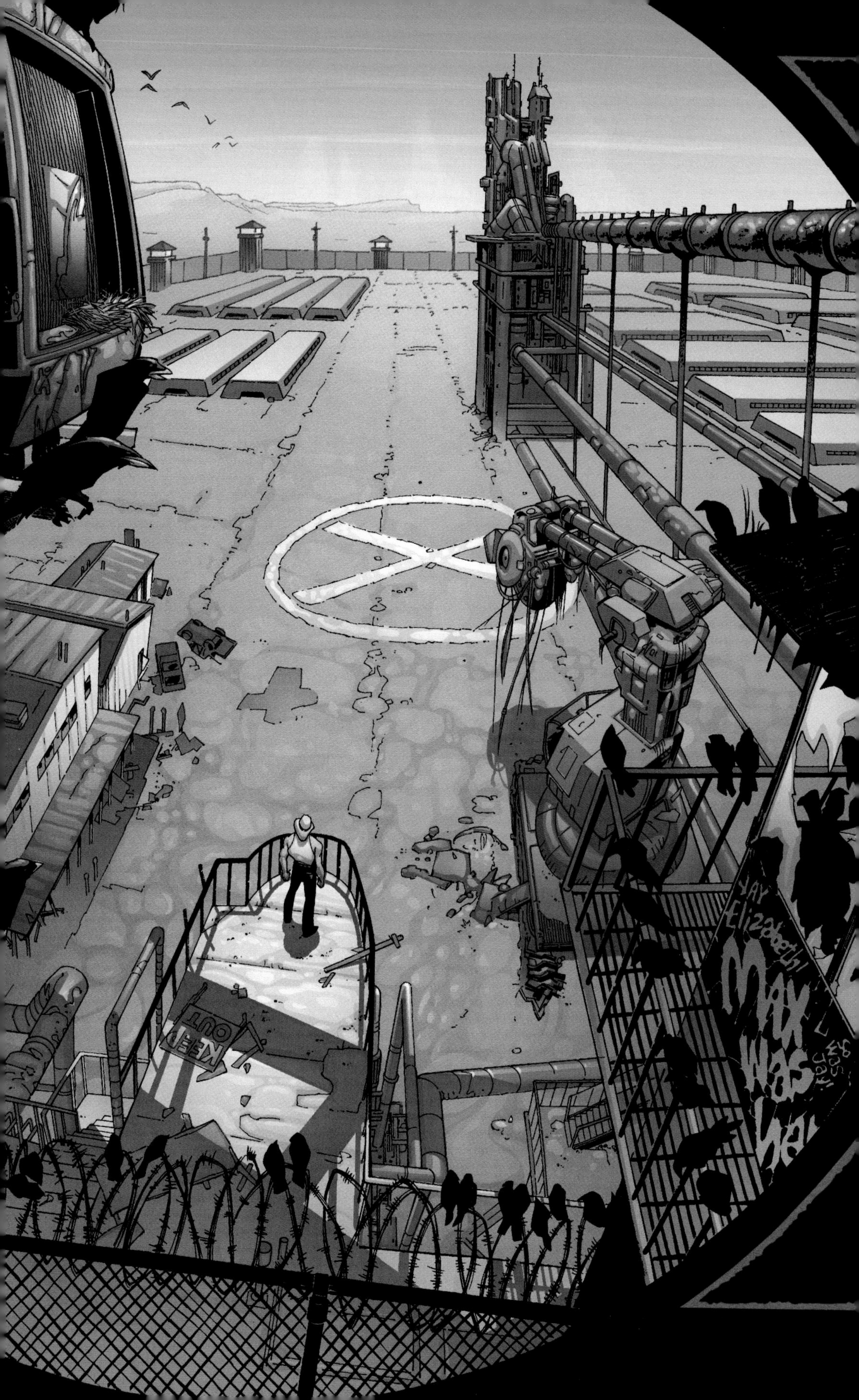
KEEP OUT
YAY Elizabeth!!
Max was here
was Jay!

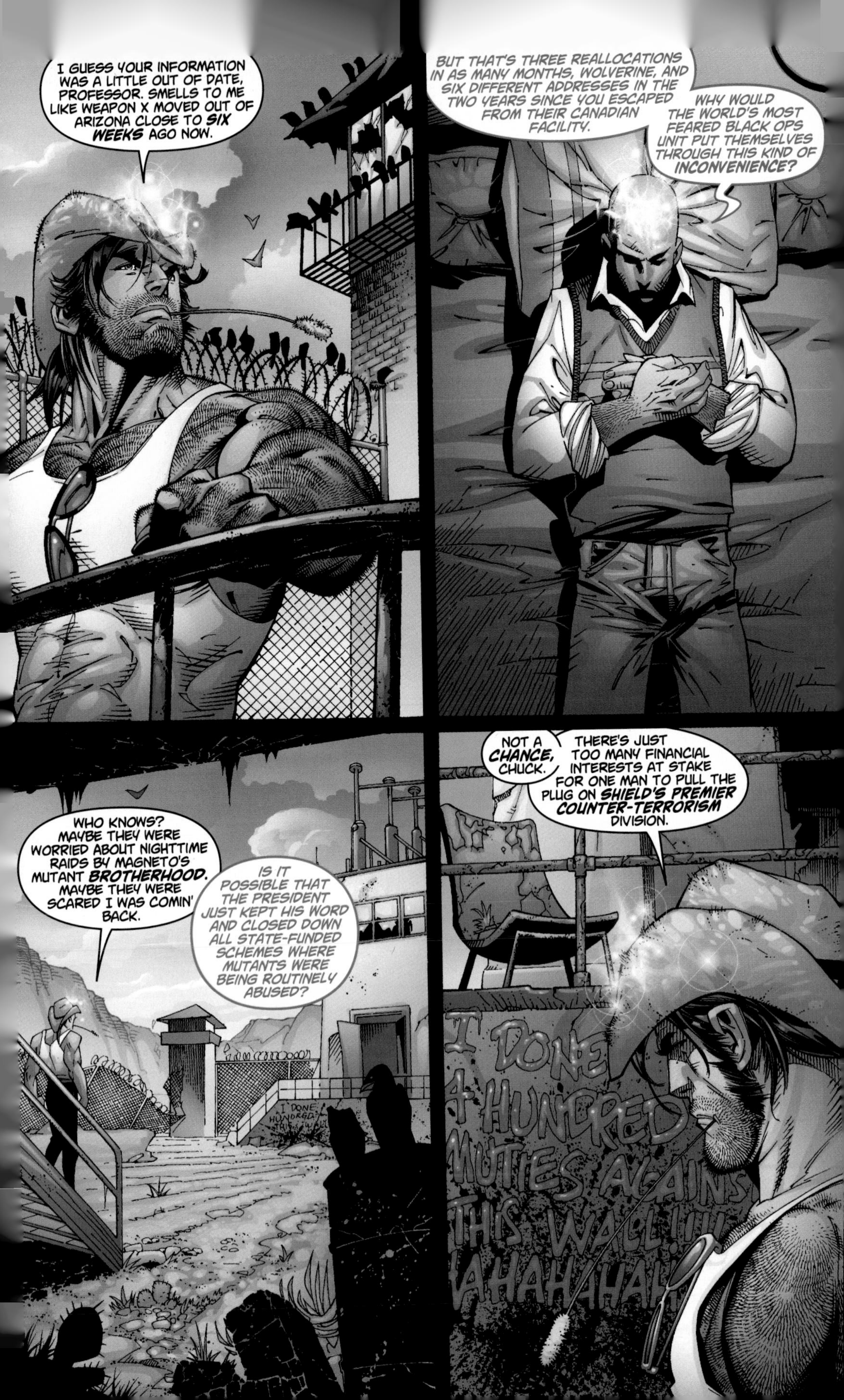

I GUESS YOUR INFORMATION WAS A LITTLE OUT OF DATE, PROFESSOR. SMELLS TO ME LIKE WEAPON X MOVED OUT OF ARIZONA CLOSE TO SIX WEEKS AGO NOW.
BUT THAT'S THREE REALLOCATIONS IN AS MANY MONTHS, WOLVERINE, AND SIX DIFFERENT ADDRESSES IN THE TWO YEARS SINCE YOU ESCAPED FROM THEIR CANADIAN FACILITY.
WHY WOULD THE WORLD'S MOST FEARED BLACK OPS UNIT PUT THEMSELVES THROUGH THIS KIND OF INCONVENIENCE?
WHO KNOWS? MAYBE THEY WERE WORRIED ABOUT NIGHTTIME RAIDS BY MAGNETO'S MUTANT BROTHERHOOD. MAYBE THEY WERE SCARED I WAS COMIN' BACK.
IS IT POSSIBLE THAT THE PRESIDENT JUST KEPT HIS WORD AND CLOSED DOWN ALL STATE-FUNDED SCHEMES WHERE MUTANTS WERE BEING ROUTINELY ABUSED?
NOT A CHANCE, CHUCK.
THERE'S JUST TOO MANY FINANCIAL INTERESTS AT STAKE FOR ONE MAN TO PULL THE PLUG ON SHIELD'S PREMIER COUNTER-TERRORISM DIVISION.
I DONE 4 HUNDRED MUTIES AGAINS THIS WALL!!! AHAHAHAH!

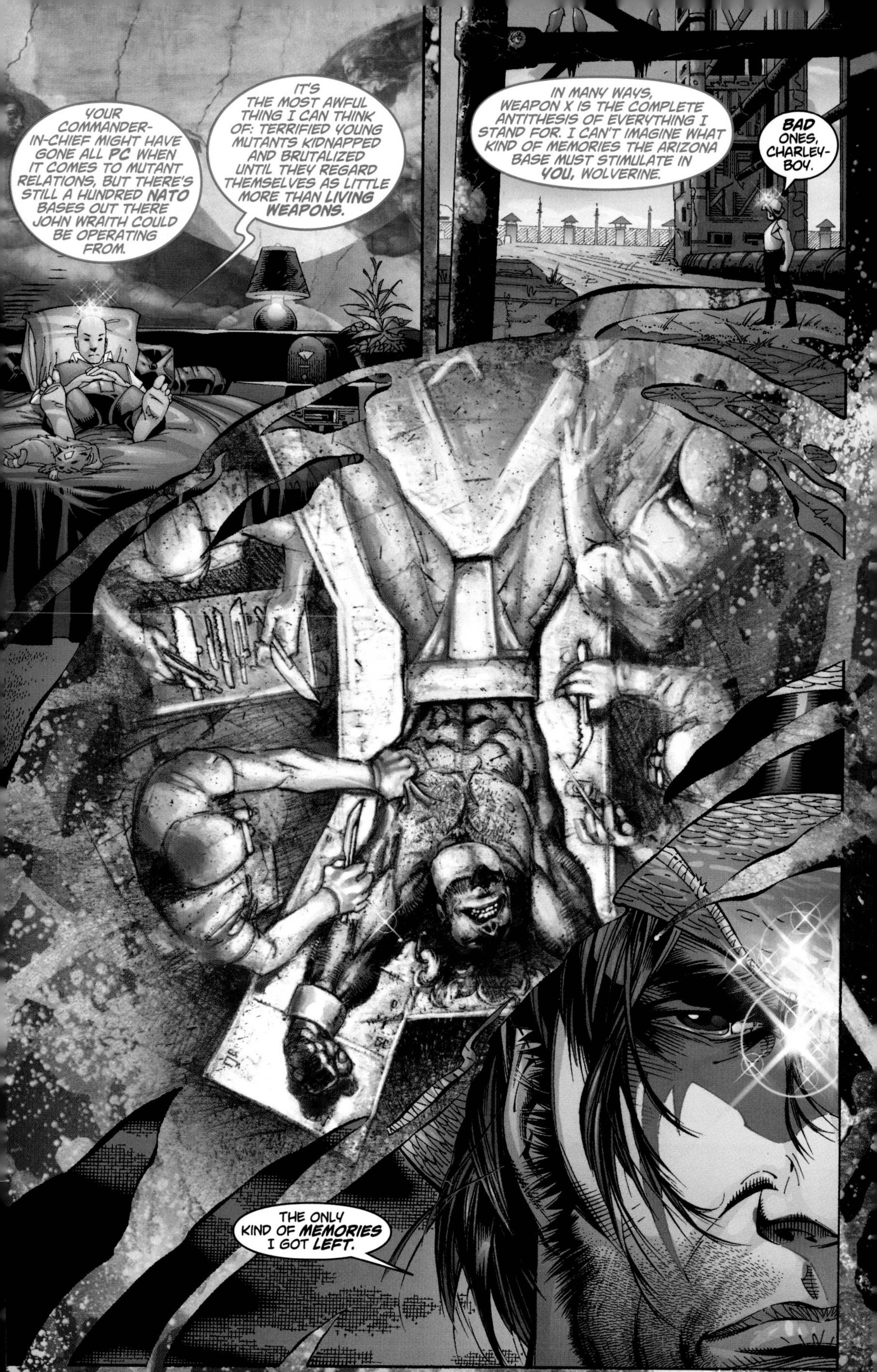
YOUR COMMANDER-IN-CHIEF MIGHT HAVE GONE ALL PC WHEN IT COMES TO MUTANT RELATIONS, BUT THERE'S STILL A HUNDRED NATO BASES OUT THERE JOHN WRAITH COULD BE OPERATING FROM.
IT'S THE MOST AWFUL THING I CAN THINK OF: TERRIFIED YOUNG MUTANTS KIDNAPPED AND BRUTALIZED UNTIL THEY REGARD THEMSELVES AS LITTLE MORE THAN LIVING WEAPONS.
IN MANY WAYS, WEAPON X IS THE COMPLETE ANTITHESIS OF EVERYTHING I STAND FOR. I CAN'T IMAGINE WHAT KIND OF MEMORIES THE ARIZONA BASE MUST STIMULATE IN YOU, WOLVERINE.
BAD ONES, CHARLEY-BOY.
THE ONLY KIND OF MEMORIES I GOT LEFT.

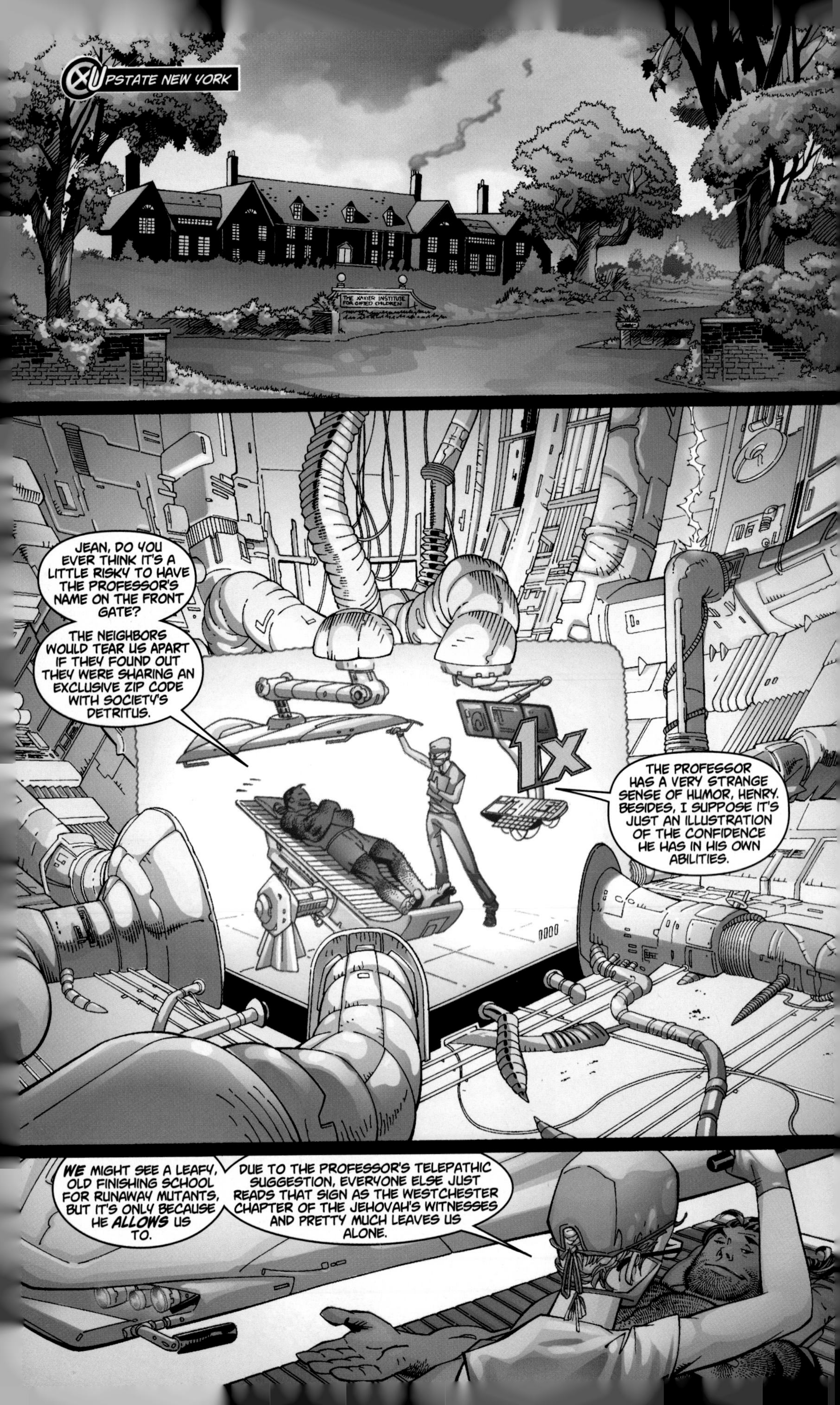
UPSTATE NEW YORK
THE XAVIER INSTITUTE FOR GIFTED CHILDREN
JEAN, DO YOU EVER THINK IT'S A LITTLE RISKY TO HAVE THE PROFESSOR'S NAME ON THE FRONT GATE?
THE NEIGHBORS WOULD TEAR US APART IF THEY FOUND OUT THEY WERE SHARING AN EXCLUSIVE ZIP CODE WITH SOCIETY'S DETRITUS.
1X
THE PROFESSOR HAS A VERY STRANGE SENSE OF HUMOR, HENRY. BESIDES, I SUPPOSE IT'S JUST AN ILLUSTRATION OF THE CONFIDENCE HE HAS IN HIS OWN ABILITIES.
WE MIGHT SEE A LEAFY, OLD FINISHING SCHOOL FOR RUNAWAY MUTANTS, BUT IT'S ONLY BECAUSE HE ALLOWS US TO.
DUE TO THE PROFESSOR'S TELEPATHIC SUGGESTION, EVERYONE ELSE JUST READS THAT SIGN AS THE WESTCHESTER CHAPTER OF THE JEHOVAH'S WITNESSES AND PRETTY MUCH LEAVES US ALONE.

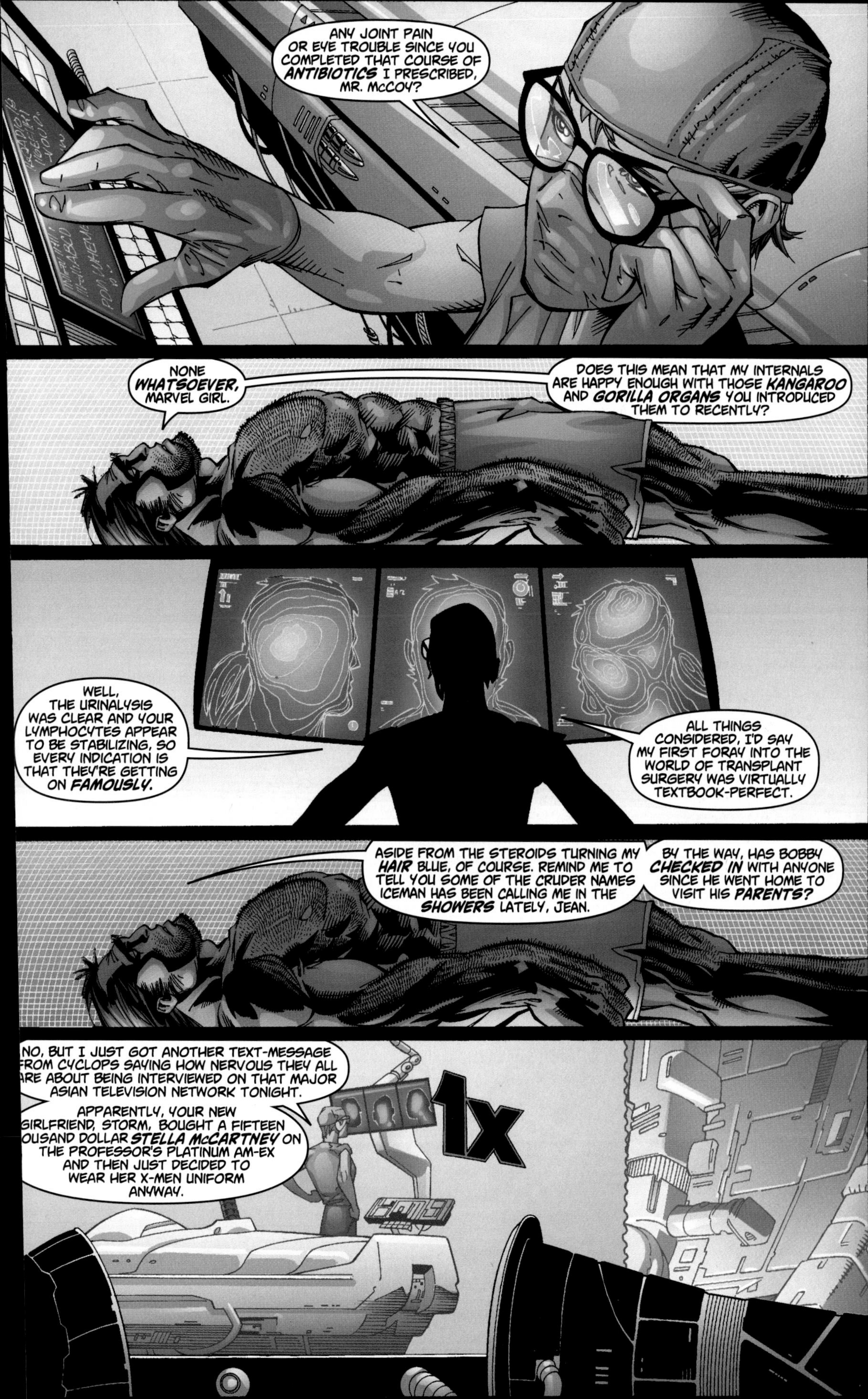
ANY JOINT PAIN OR EYE TROUBLE SINCE YOU COMPLETED THAT COURSE OF ANTIBIOTICS I PRESCRIBED, MR. McCOY?
NONE WHATSOEVER, MARVEL GIRL.
DOES THIS MEAN THAT MY INTERNALS ARE HAPPY ENOUGH WITH THOSE KANGAROO AND GORILLA ORGANS YOU INTRODUCED THEM TO RECENTLY?
WELL, THE URINALYSIS WAS CLEAR AND YOUR LYMPHOCYTES APPEAR TO BE STABILIZING, SO EVERY INDICATION IS THAT THEY'RE GETTING ON FAMOUSLY.
ALL THINGS CONSIDERED, I'D SAY MY FIRST FORAY INTO THE WORLD OF TRANSPLANT SURGERY WAS VIRTUALLY TEXTBOOK-PERFECT.
ASIDE FROM THE STEROIDS TURNING MY HAIR BLUE, OF COURSE. REMIND ME TO TELL YOU SOME OF THE CRUDER NAMES ICEMAN HAS BEEN CALLING ME IN THE SHOWERS LATELY, JEAN.
BY THE WAY, HAS BOBBY CHECKED IN WITH ANYONE SINCE HE WENT HOME TO VISIT HIS PARENTS?
NO, BUT I JUST GOT ANOTHER TEXT-MESSAGE FROM CYCLOPS SAYING HOW NERVOUS THEY ALL ARE ABOUT BEING INTERVIEWED ON THAT MAJOR ASIAN TELEVISION NETWORK TONIGHT.
APPARENTLY, YOUR NEW GIRLFRIEND, STORM, BOUGHT A FIFTEEN THOUSAND DOLLAR STELLA McCARTNEY ON THE PROFESSOR'S PLATINUM AM-EX AND THEN JUST DECIDED TO WEAR HER X-MEN UNIFORM ANYWAY.
1X

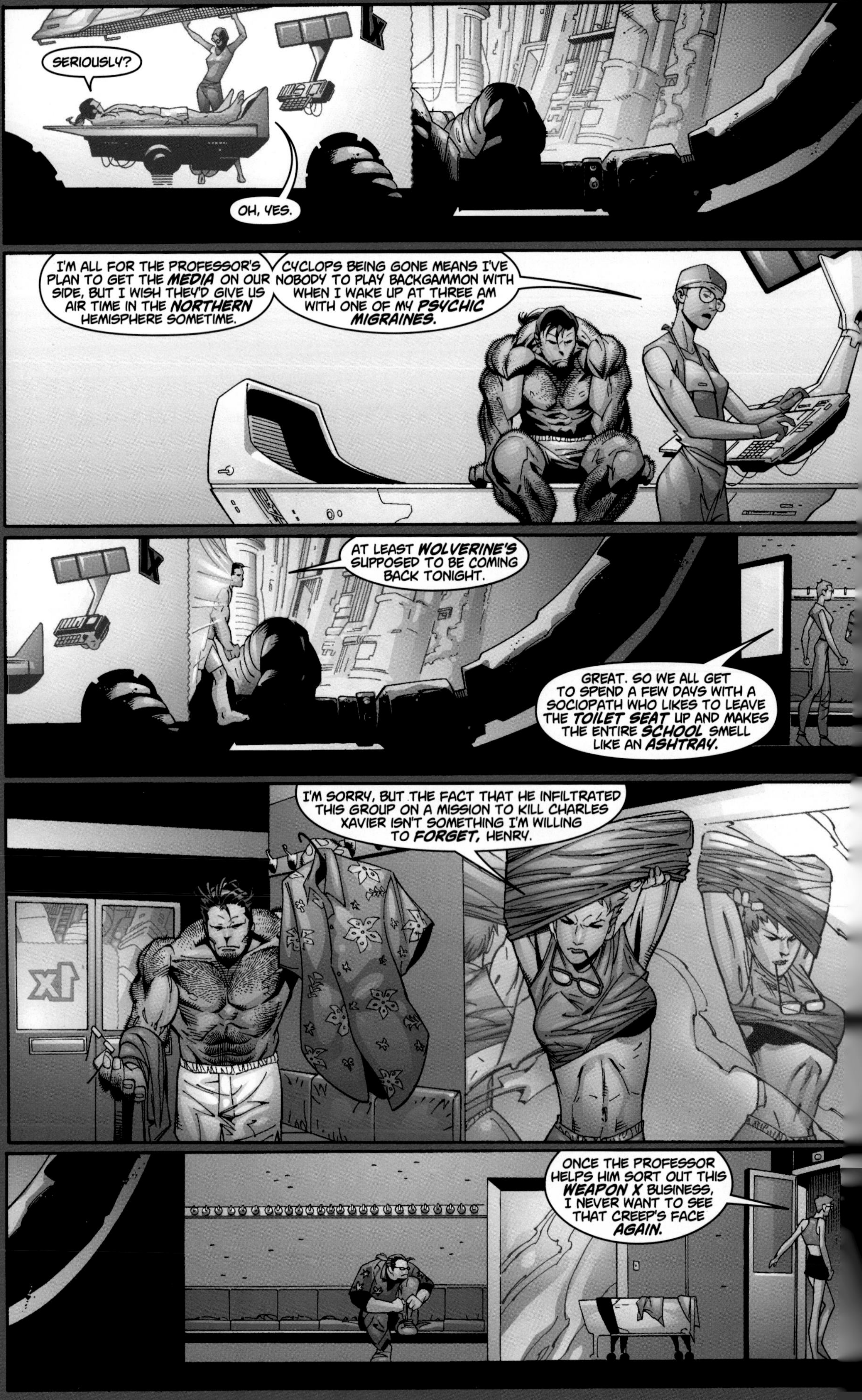
SERIOUSLY?
OH, YES.
I'M ALL FOR THE PROFESSOR'S PLAN TO GET THE MEDIA ON OUR SIDE, BUT I WISH THEY'D GIVE US AIR TIME IN THE NORTHERN HEMISPHERE SOMETIME.
CYCLOPS BEING GONE MEANS I'VE NOBODY TO PLAY BACKGAMMON WITH WHEN I WAKE UP AT THREE AM WITH ONE OF MY PSYCHIC MIGRAINES.
AT LEAST WOLVERINE'S SUPPOSED TO BE COMING BACK TONIGHT.
GREAT. SO WE ALL GET TO SPEND A FEW DAYS WITH A SOCIOPATH WHO LIKES TO LEAVE THE TOILET SEAT UP AND MAKES THE ENTIRE SCHOOL SMELL LIKE AN ASHTRAY.
I'M SORRY, BUT THE FACT THAT HE INFILTRATED THIS GROUP ON A MISSION TO KILL CHARLES XAVIER ISN'T SOMETHING I'M WILLING TO FORGET, HENRY.
ONCE THE PROFESSOR HELPS HIM SORT OUT THIS WEAPON X BUSINESS, I NEVER WANT TO SEE THAT CREEP'S FACE AGAIN.

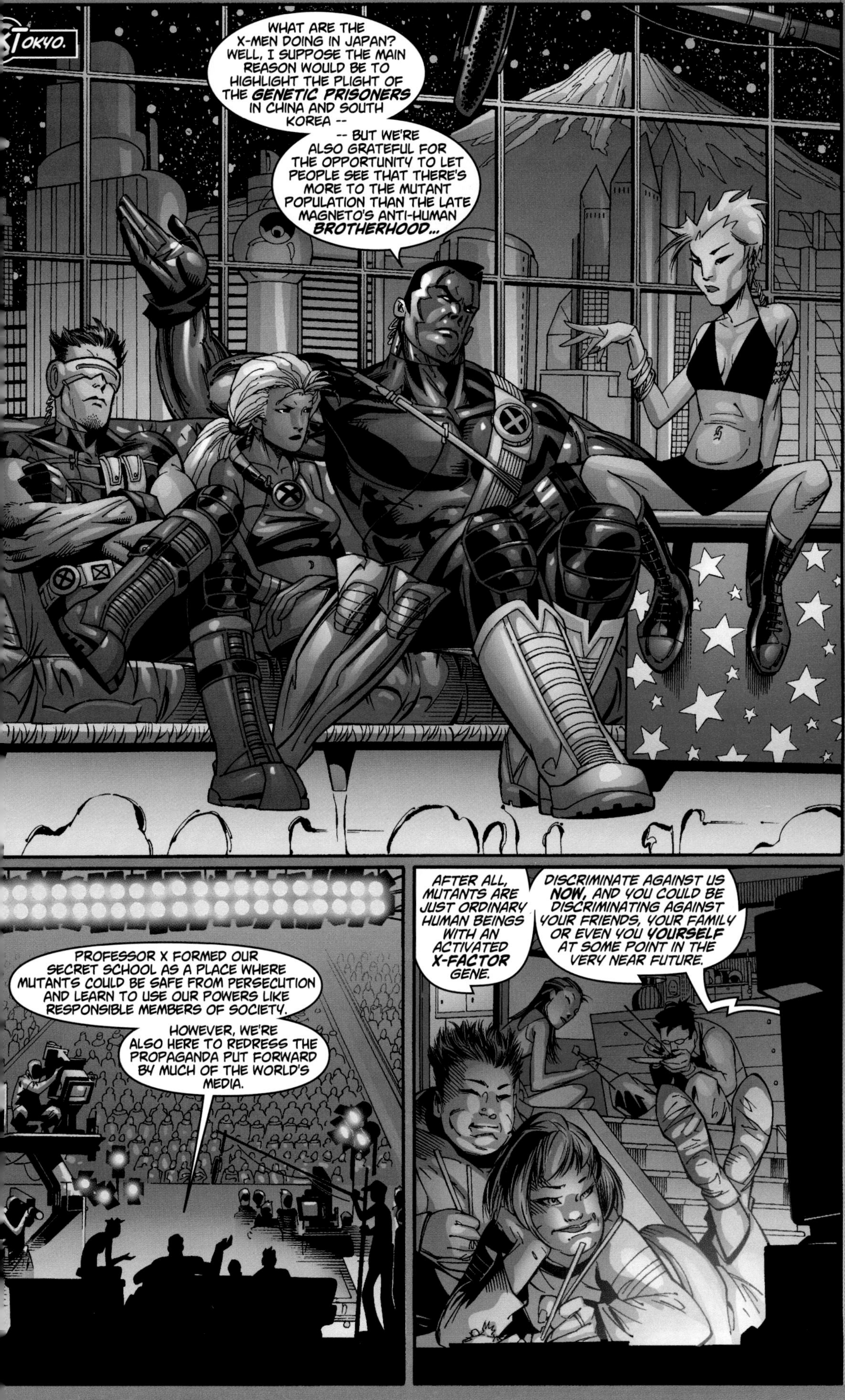
TOKYO.
WHAT ARE THE X-MEN DOING IN JAPAN? WELL, I SUPPOSE THE MAIN REASON WOULD BE TO HIGHLIGHT THE PLIGHT OF THE GENETIC PRISONERS IN CHINA AND SOUTH KOREA --
-- BUT WE'RE ALSO GRATEFUL FOR THE OPPORTUNITY TO LET PEOPLE SEE THAT THERE'S MORE TO THE MUTANT POPULATION THAN THE LATE MAGNETO'S ANTI-HUMAN BROTHERHOOD...
PROFESSOR X FORMED OUR SECRET SCHOOL AS A PLACE WHERE MUTANTS COULD BE SAFE FROM PERSECUTION AND LEARN TO USE OUR POWERS LIKE RESPONSIBLE MEMBERS OF SOCIETY.
HOWEVER, WE'RE ALSO HERE TO REDRESS THE PROPAGANDA PUT FORWARD BY MUCH OF THE WORLD'S MEDIA.
AFTER ALL, MUTANTS ARE JUST ORDINARY HUMAN BEINGS WITH AN ACTIVATED X-FACTOR GENE.
DISCRIMINATE AGAINST US NOW, AND YOU COULD BE DISCRIMINATING AGAINST YOUR FRIENDS, YOUR FAMILY OR EVEN YOU YOURSELF AT SOME POINT IN THE VERY NEAR FUTURE.

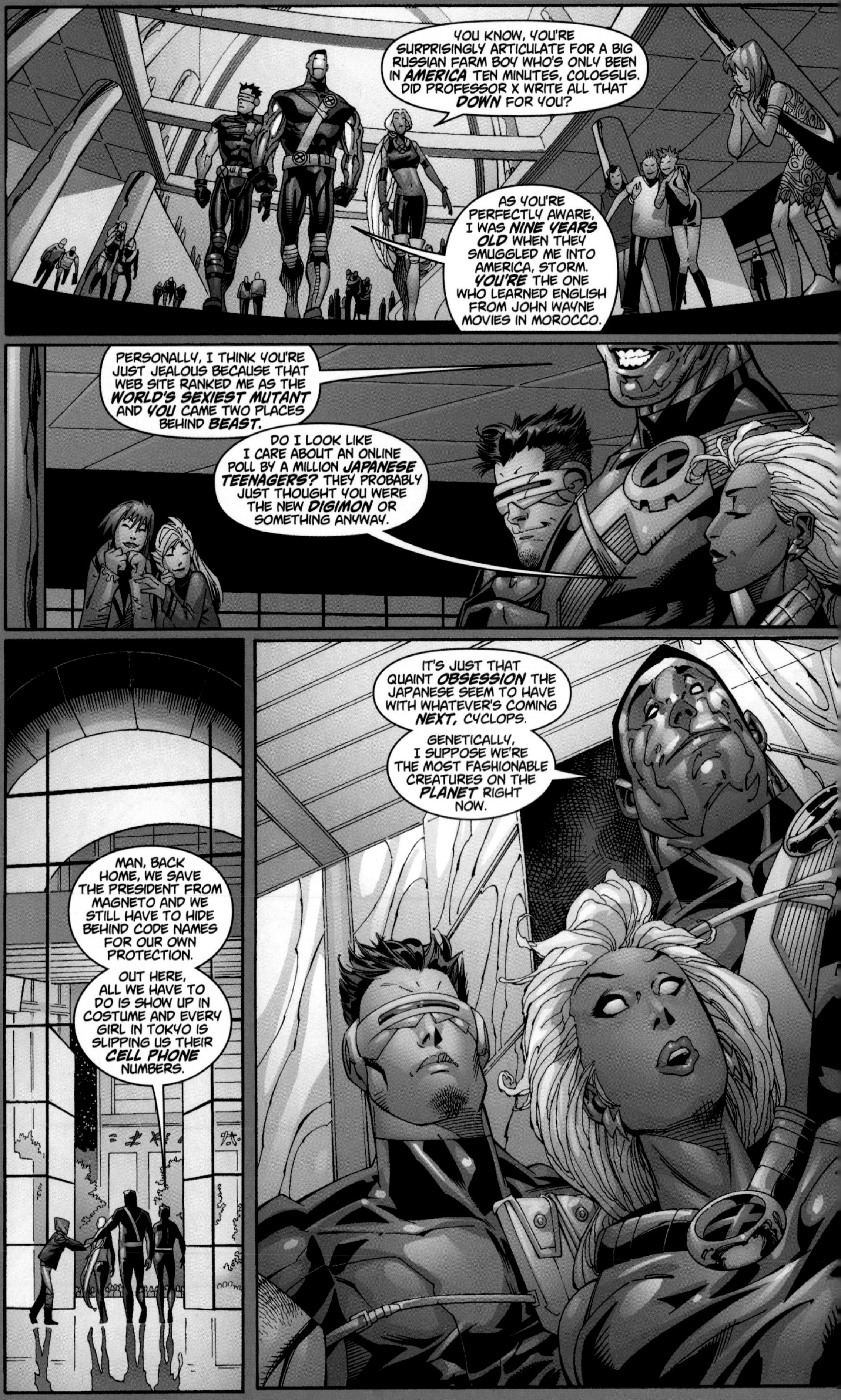
YOU KNOW, YOU'RE SURPRISINGLY ARTICULATE FOR A BIG RUSSIAN FARM BOY WHO'S ONLY BEEN IN AMERICA TEN MINUTES, COLOSSUS. DID PROFESSOR X WRITE ALL THAT DOWN FOR YOU?
AS YOU'RE PERFECTLY AWARE, I WAS NINE YEARS OLD WHEN THEY SMUGGLED ME INTO AMERICA, STORM. YOU'RE THE ONE WHO LEARNED ENGLISH FROM JOHN WAYNE MOVIES IN MOROCCO.
PERSONALLY, I THINK YOU'RE JUST JEALOUS BECAUSE THAT WEB SITE RANKED ME AS THE WORLD'S SEXIEST MUTANT AND YOU CAME TWO PLACES BEHIND BEAST.
DO I LOOK LIKE I CARE ABOUT AN ONLINE POLL BY A MILLION JAPANESE TEENAGERS? THEY PROBABLY JUST THOUGHT YOU WERE THE NEW DIGIMON OR SOMETHING ANYWAY.
MAN, BACK HOME, WE SAVE THE PRESIDENT FROM MAGNETO AND WE STILL HAVE TO HIDE BEHIND CODE NAMES FOR OUR OWN PROTECTION.
OUT HERE, ALL WE HAVE TO DO IS SHOW UP IN COSTUME AND EVERY GIRL IN TOKYO IS SLIPPING US THEIR CELL PHONE NUMBERS.
IT'S JUST THAT QUAINT OBSESSION THE JAPANESE SEEM TO HAVE WITH WHATEVER'S COMING NEXT, CYCLOPS.
GENETICALLY, I SUPPOSE WE'RE THE MOST FASHIONABLE CREATURES ON THE PLANET RIGHT NOW.

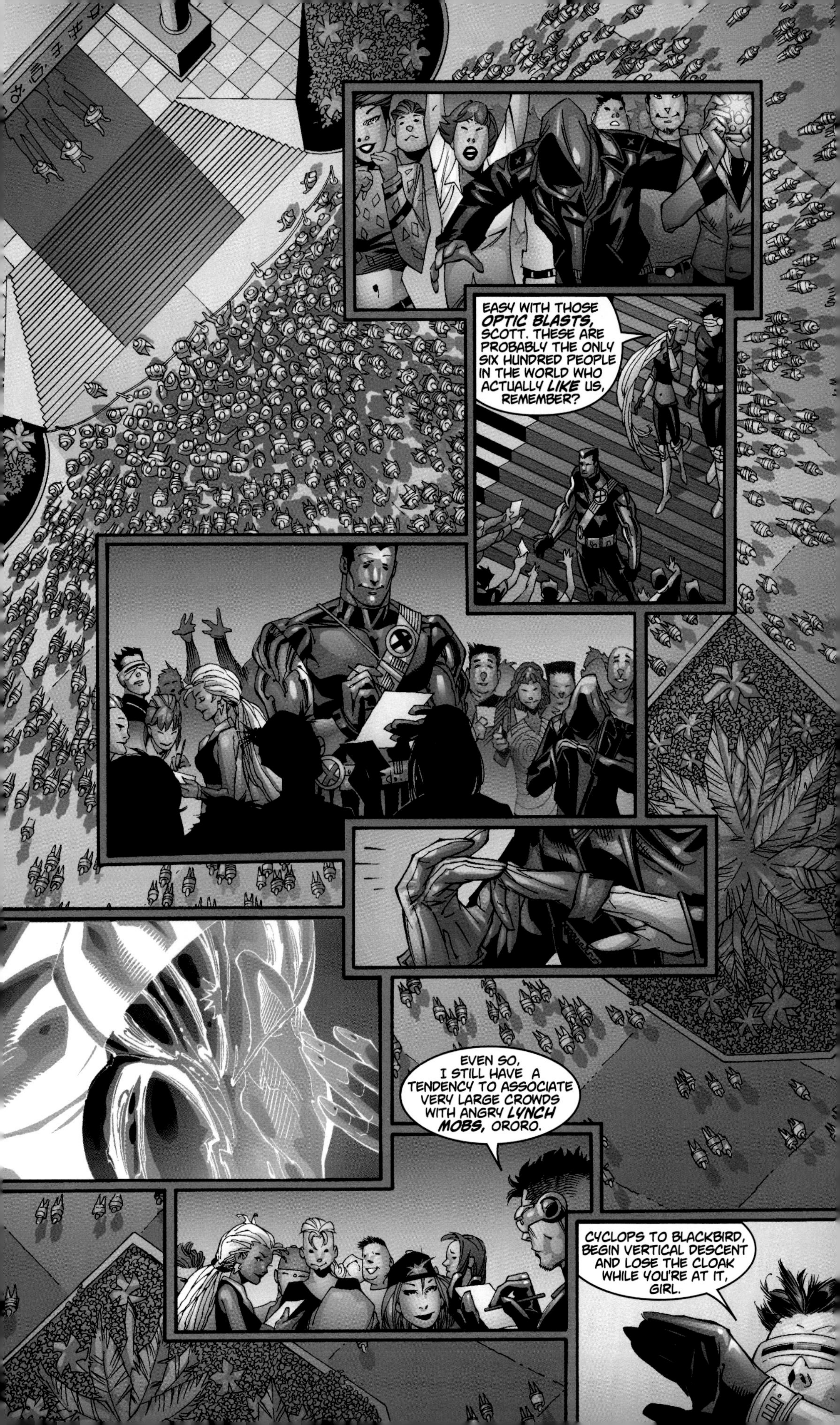
EASY WITH THOSE OPTIC BLASTS, SCOTT. THESE ARE PROBABLY THE ONLY SIX HUNDRED PEOPLE IN THE WORLD WHO ACTUALLY LIKE US, REMEMBER?
EVEN SO, I STILL HAVE A TENDENCY TO ASSOCIATE VERY LARGE CROWDS WITH ANGRY LYNCH MOBS, ORORO.
CYCLOPS TO BLACKBIRD, BEGIN VERTICAL DESCENT AND LOSE THE CLOAK WHILE YOU'RE AT IT, GIRL.

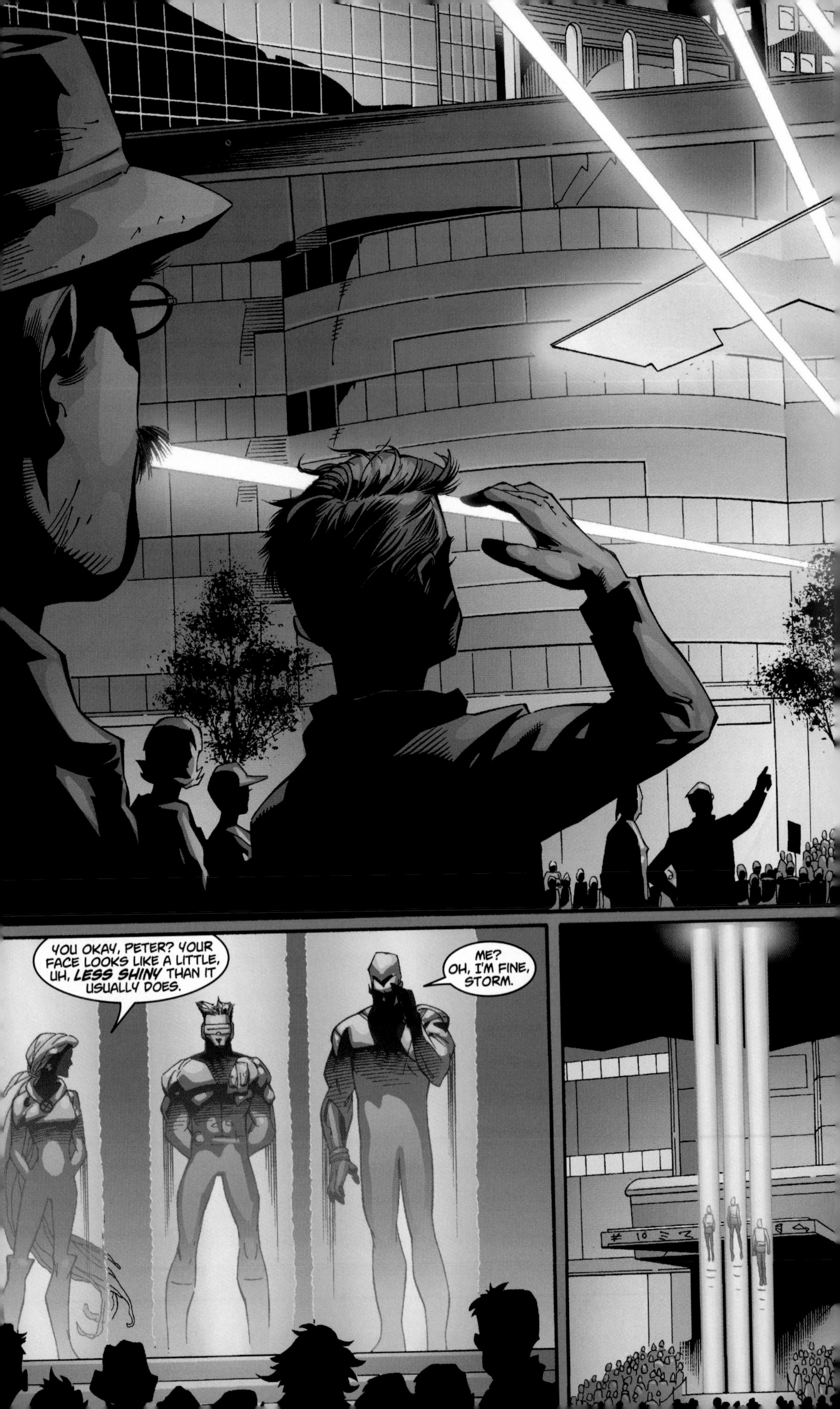
YOU OKAY, PETER? YOUR FACE LOOKS LIKE A LITTLE, UH, LESS SHINY THAN IT USUALLY DOES.
ME? OH, I'M FINE, STORM.

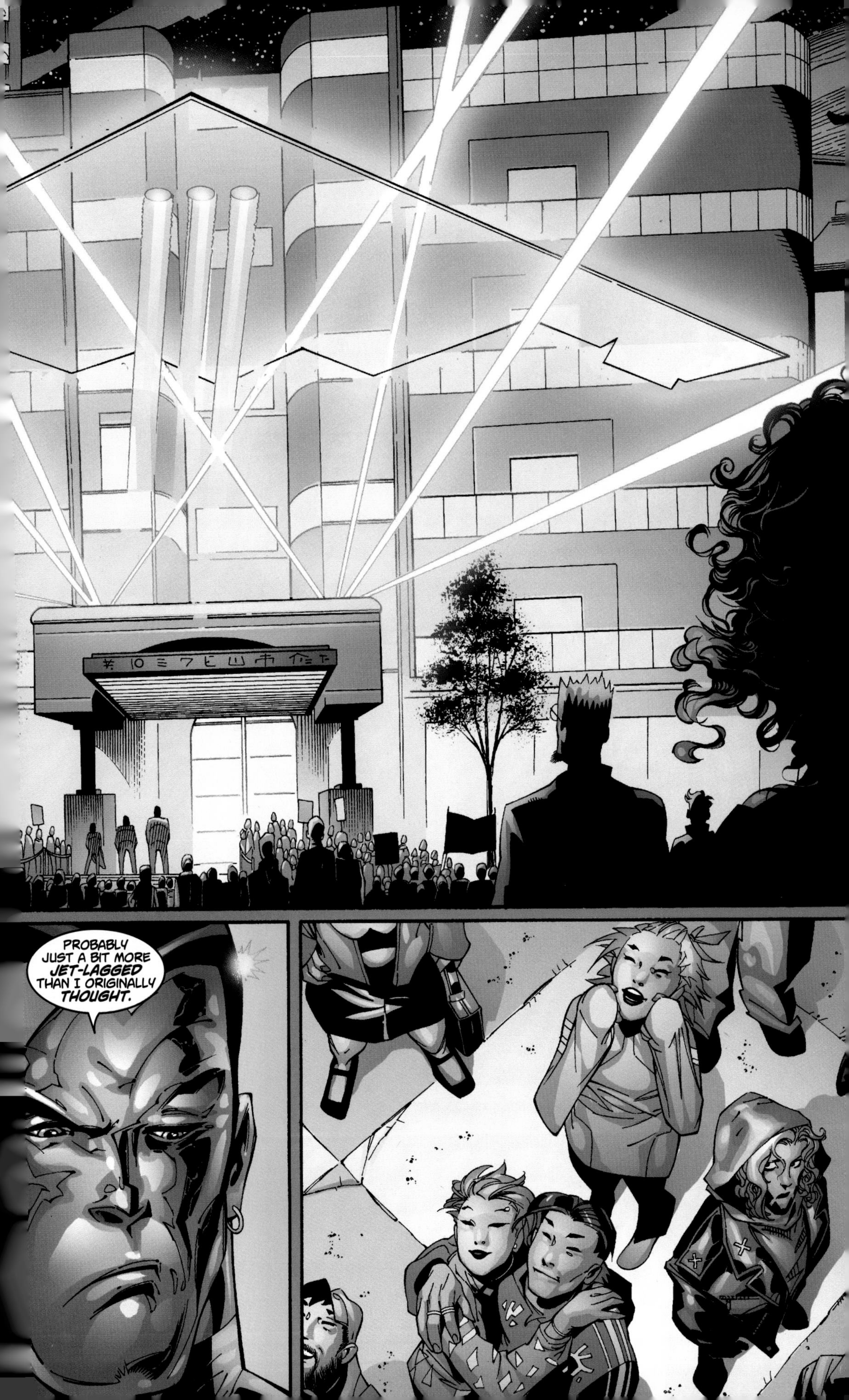
PROBABLY JUST A BIT MORE JET-LAGGED THAN I ORIGINALLY THOUGHT.

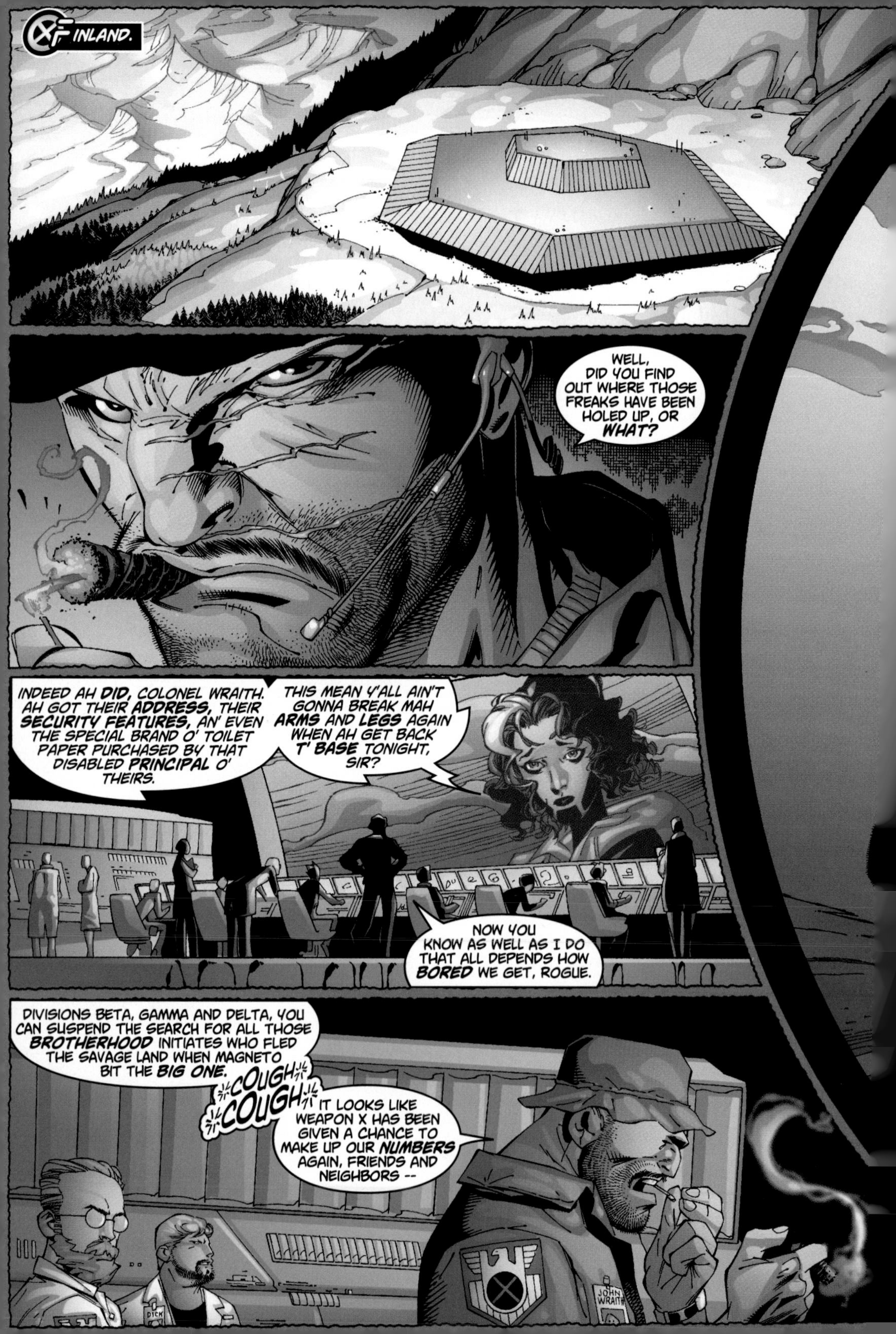
FINLAND.
WELL, DID YOU FIND OUT WHERE THOSE FREAKS HAVE BEEN HOLED UP, OR WHAT?
INDEED AH DID, COLONEL WRAITH. AH GOT THEIR ADDRESS, THEIR SECURITY FEATURES, AN' EVEN THE SPECIAL BRAND O' TOILET PAPER PURCHASED BY THAT DISABLED PRINCIPAL O' THEIRS.
THIS MEAN Y'ALL AIN'T GONNA BREAK MAH ARMS AND LEGS AGAIN WHEN AH GET BACK T' BASE TONIGHT, SIR?
NOW YOU KNOW AS WELL AS I DO THAT ALL DEPENDS HOW BORED WE GET, ROGUE.
DIVISIONS BETA, GAMMA AND DELTA, YOU CAN SUSPEND THE SEARCH FOR ALL THOSE BROTHERHOOD INITIATES WHO FLED THE SAVAGE LAND WHEN MAGNETO BIT THE BIG ONE.
COUGH COUGH
IT LOOKS LIKE WEAPON X HAS BEEN GIVEN A CHANCE TO MAKE UP OUR NUMBERS AGAIN, FRIENDS AND NEIGHBORS --
JOHN WRAITH
DICK

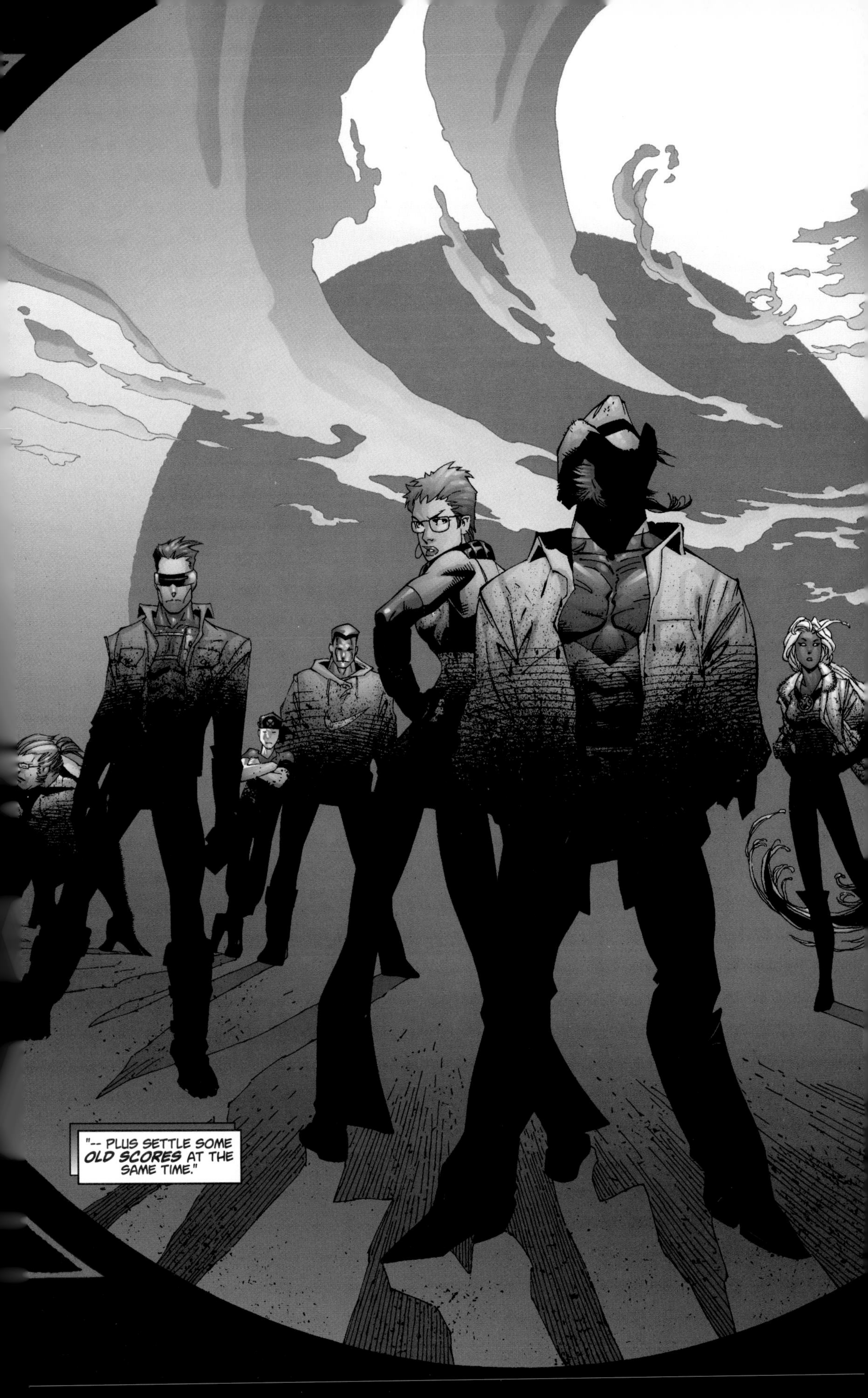
"-- PLUS SETTLE SOME OLD SCORES AT THE SAME TIME."

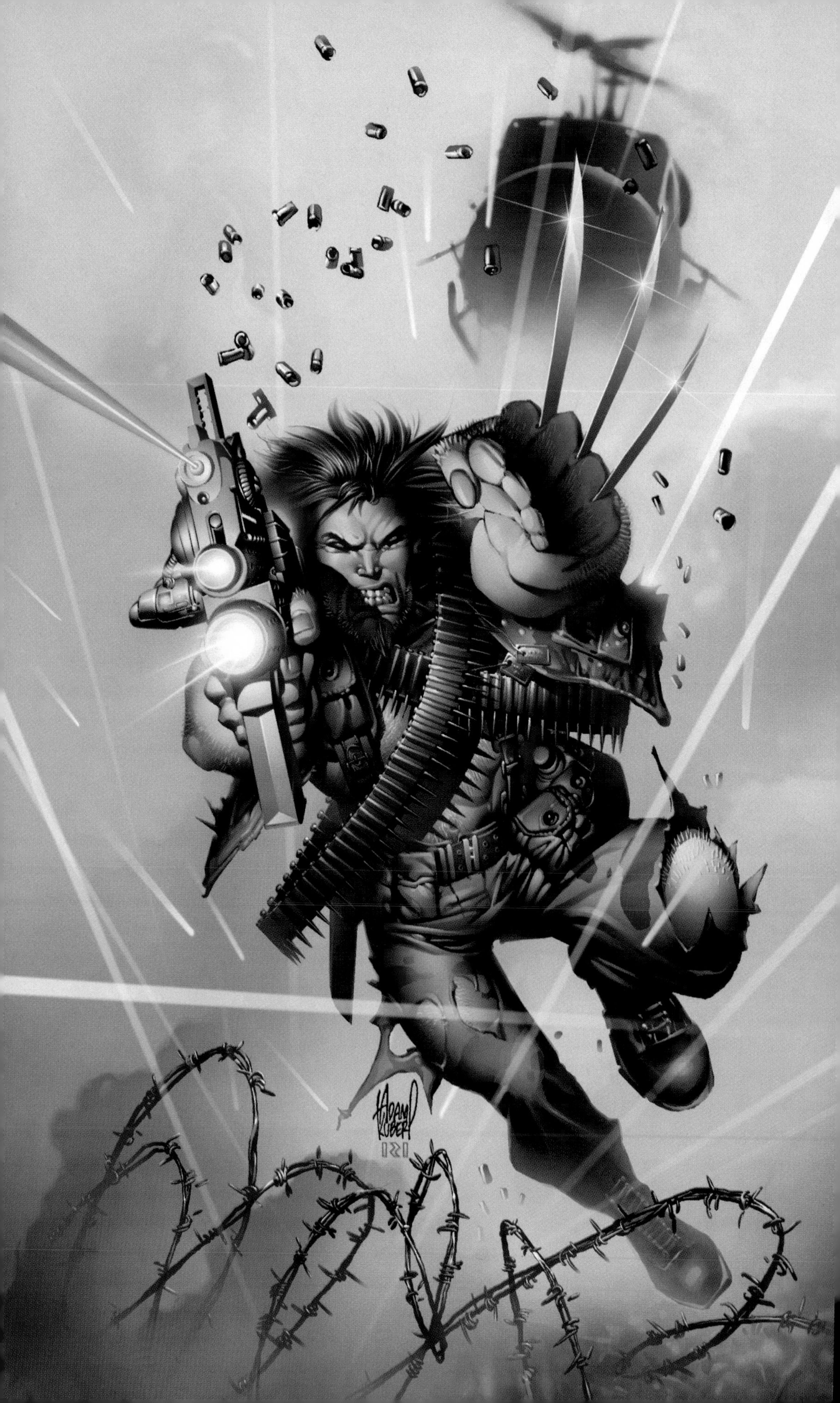
ADAM KUBERT

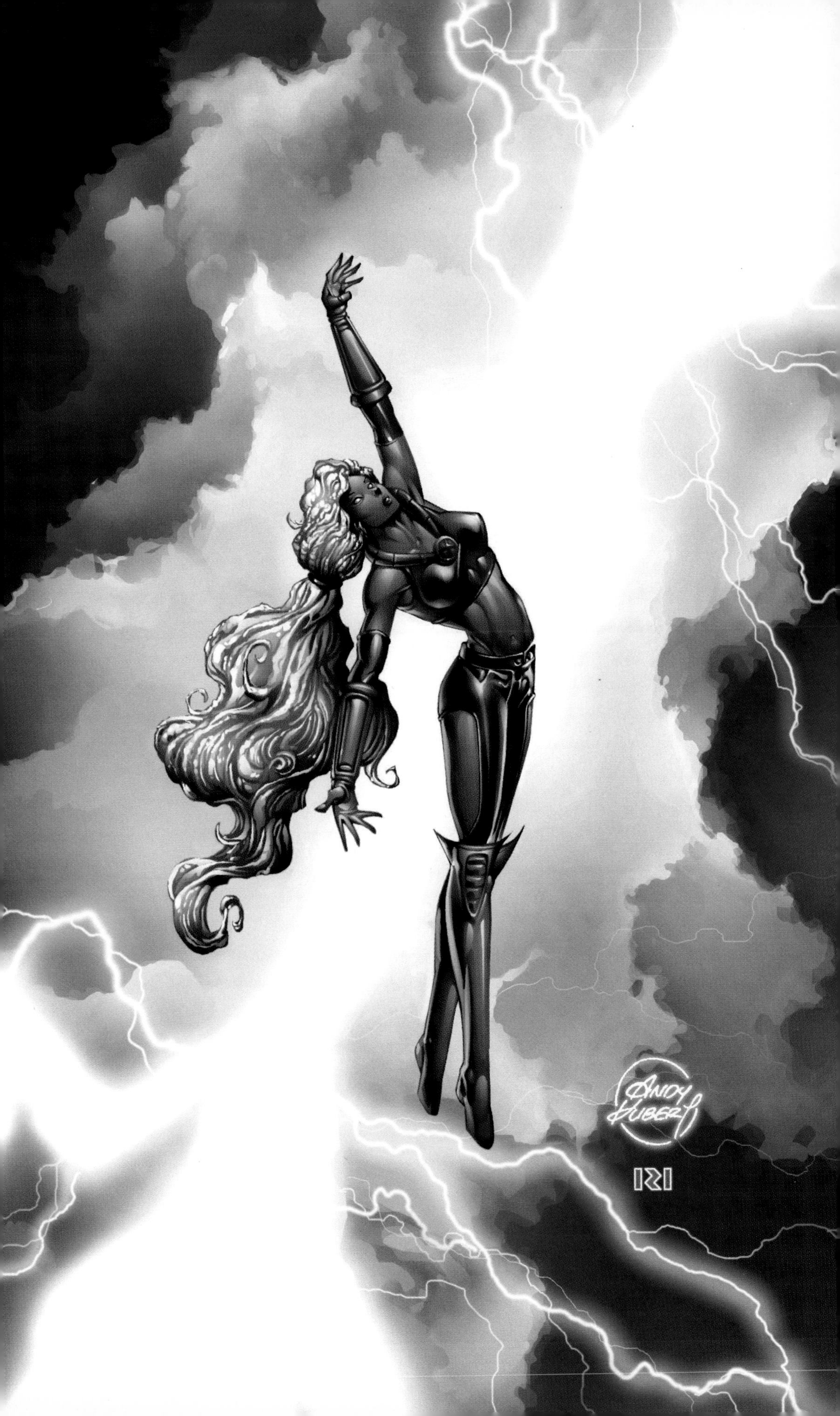

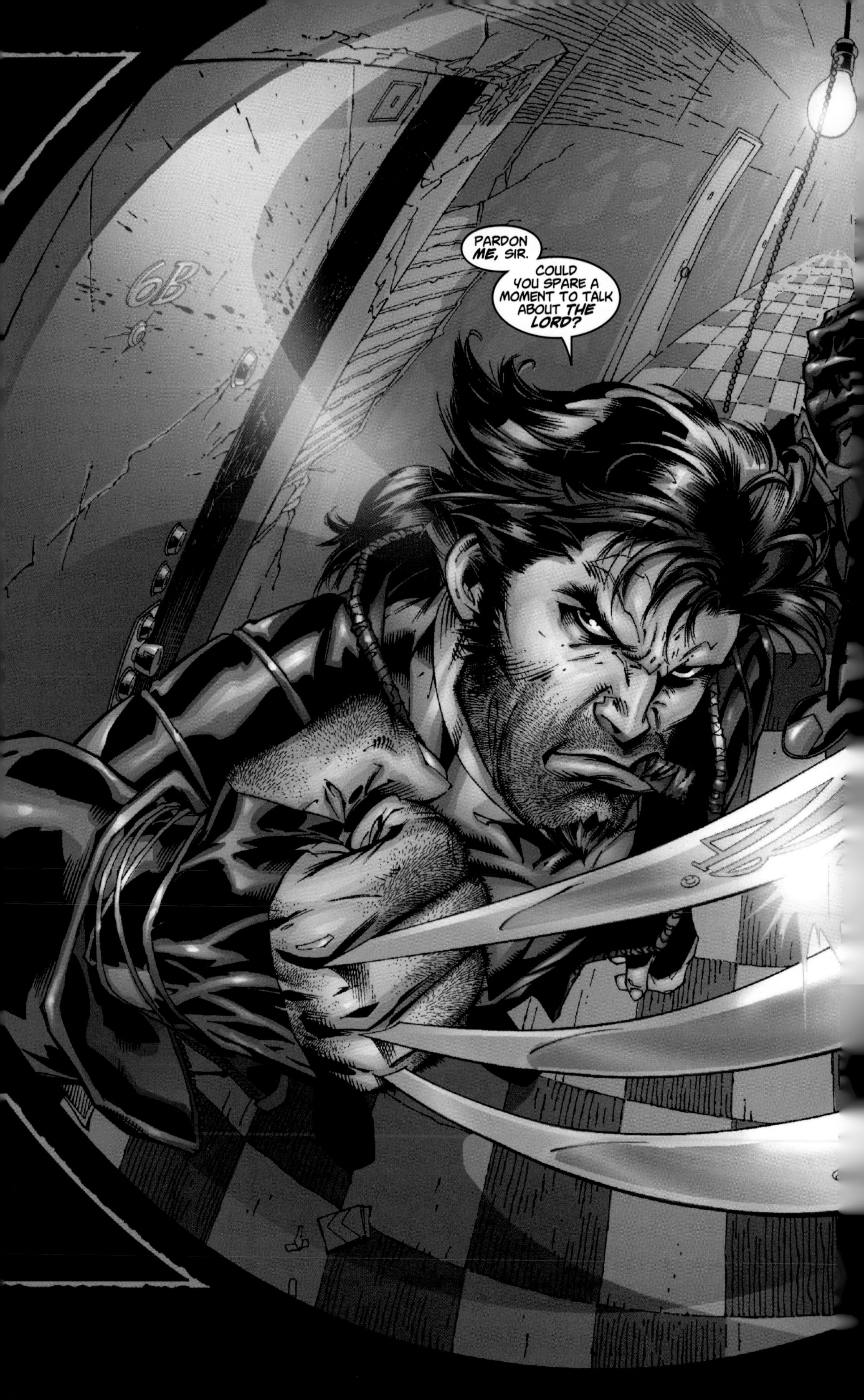
PARDON ME, SIR.
COULD YOU SPARE A MOMENT TO TALK ABOUT THE LORD?

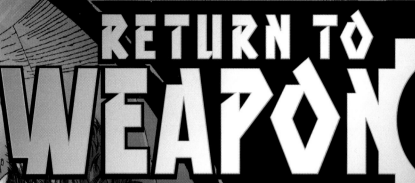

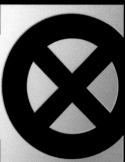

RETURN TO WEAPON X

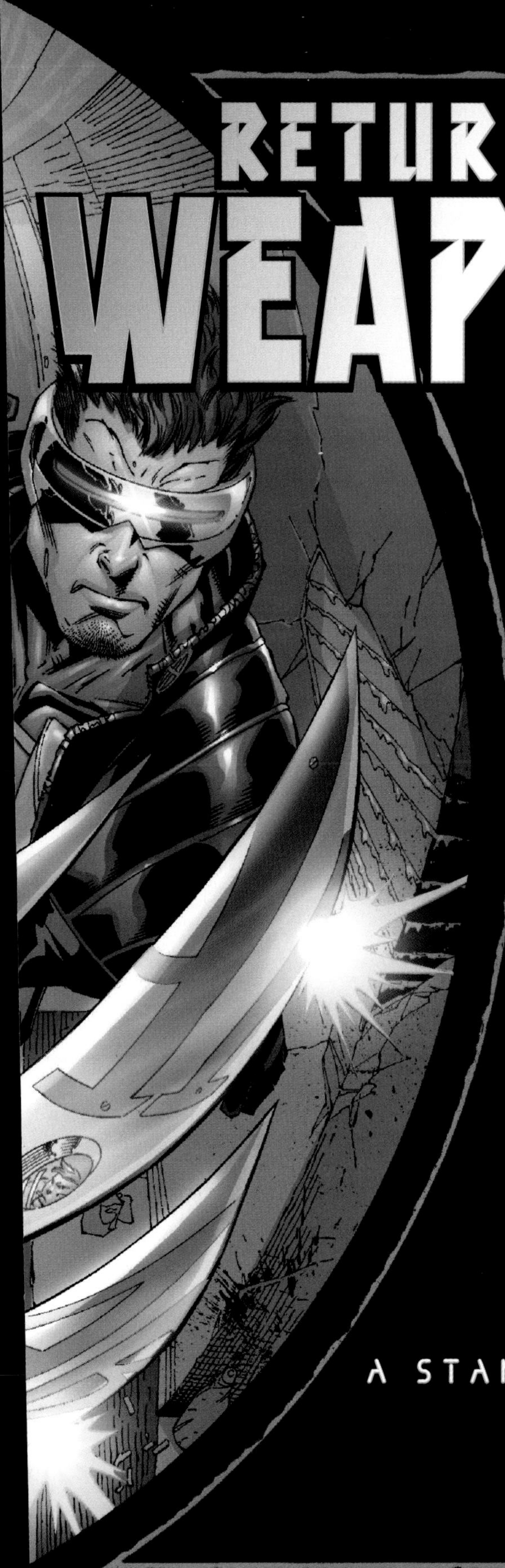

PART TWO OF SIX

MARK MILLAR
writer
ADAM KUBERT
pencils
ART THIBERT
inks
JUNG CHOI
colors
RICHARD STARKINGS
& COMICRAFT'S
WES ABBOTT
letters
PETE FRANCO
assistant editor
MARK POWERS
editor
JOE QUESADA
editor in chief
BILL JEMAS
president

A STAN LEE PRESENTATION

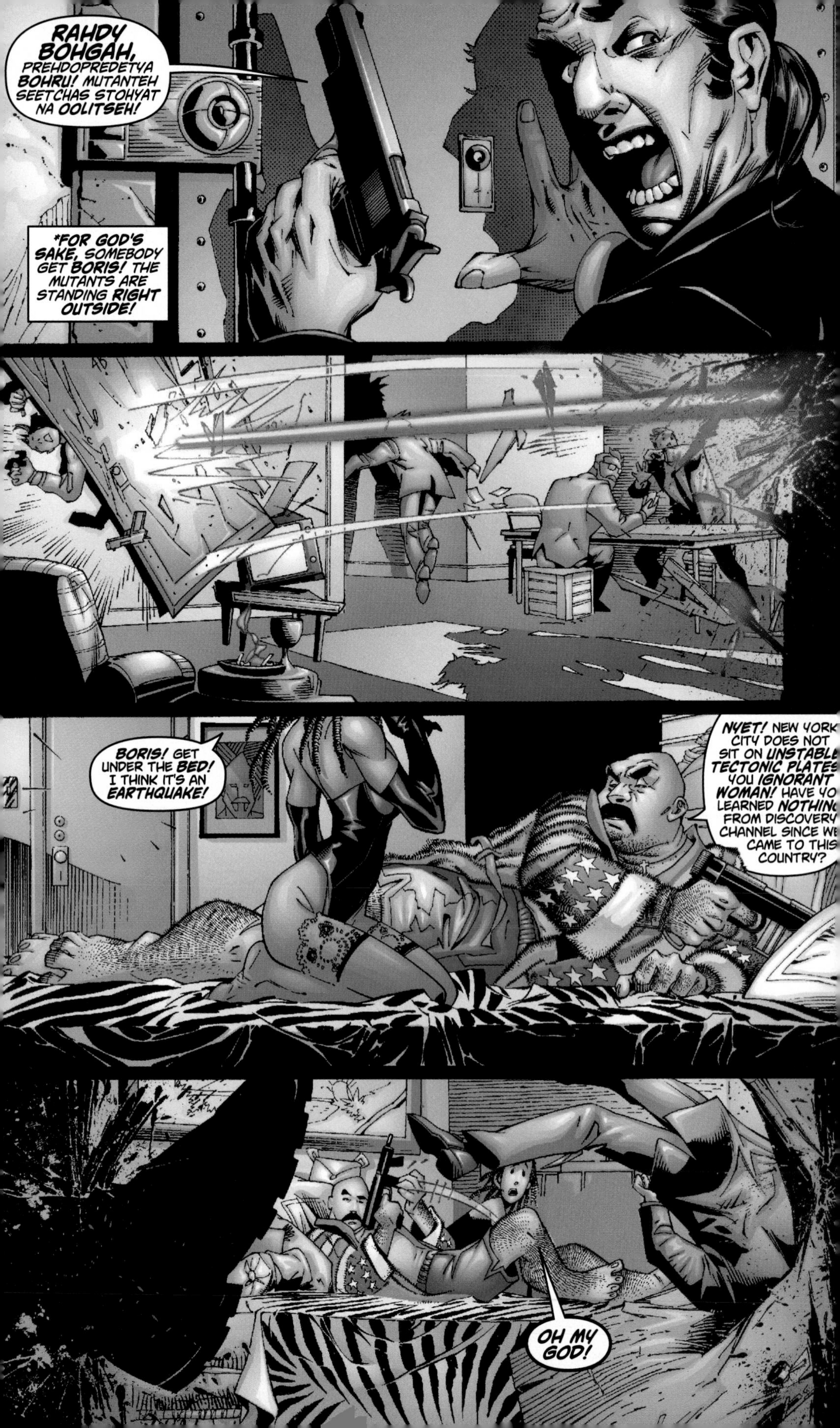
RAHDY BOHGAH, PREHDOPREDETYA BOHRU! MUTANTEH SEETCHAS STOHYAT NA OOLITSEH!
*FOR GOD'S SAKE, SOMEBODY GET BORIS! THE MUTANTS ARE STANDING RIGHT OUTSIDE!
BORIS! GET UNDER THE BED! I THINK IT'S AN EARTHQUAKE!
NYET! NEW YORK CITY DOES NOT SIT ON UNSTABLE TECTONIC PLATES YOU IGNORANT WOMAN! HAVE YO LEARNED NOTHING FROM DISCOVERY CHANNEL SINCE WE CAME TO THIS COUNTRY?
OH MY GOD!

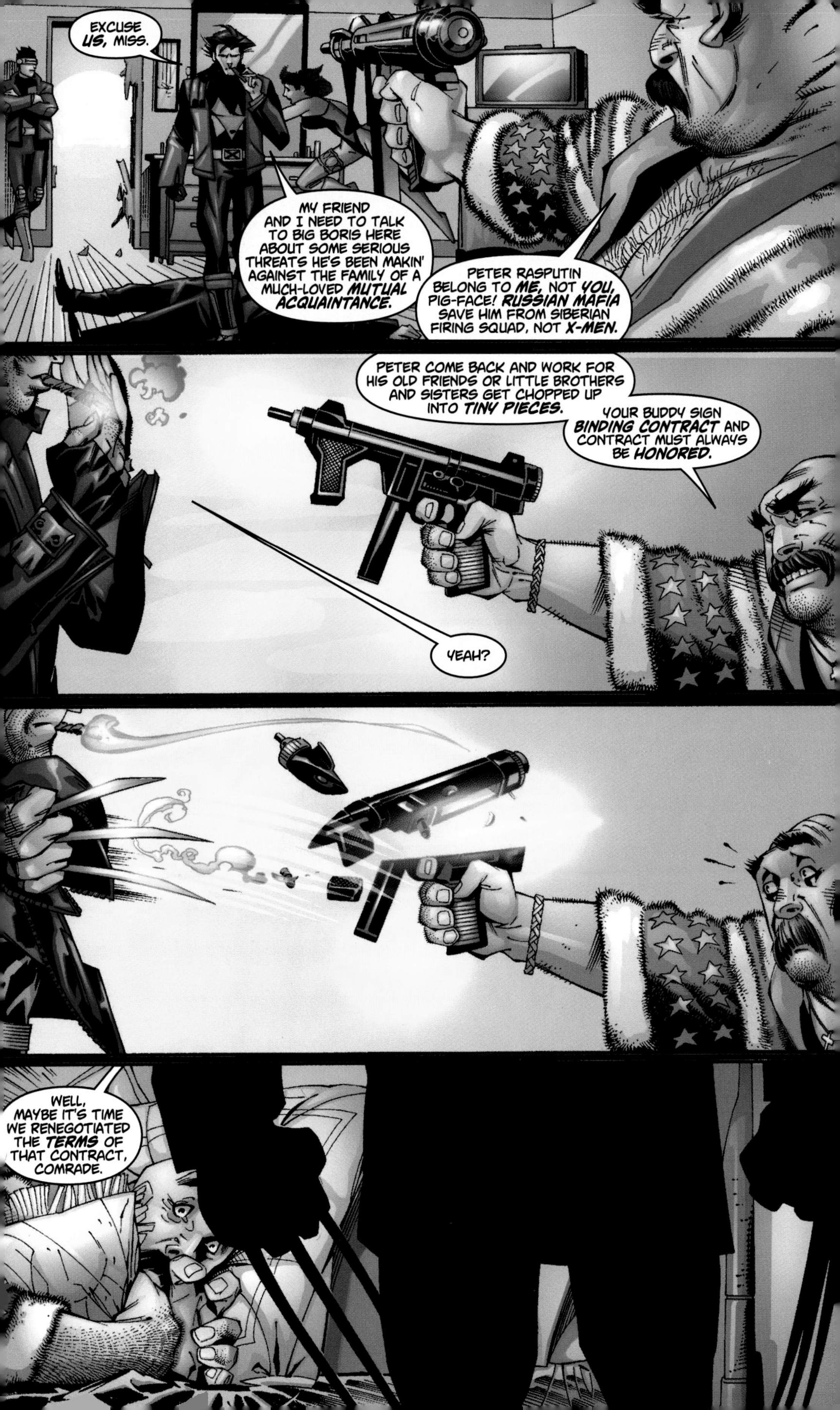
EXCUSE US, MISS.
MY FRIEND AND I NEED TO TALK TO BIG BORIS HERE ABOUT SOME SERIOUS THREATS HE'S BEEN MAKIN' AGAINST THE FAMILY OF A MUCH-LOVED MUTUAL ACQUAINTANCE.
PETER RASPUTIN BELONG TO ME, NOT YOU, PIG-FACE! RUSSIAN MAFIA SAVE HIM FROM SIBERIAN FIRING SQUAD, NOT X-MEN.
PETER COME BACK AND WORK FOR HIS OLD FRIENDS OR LITTLE BROTHERS AND SISTERS GET CHOPPED UP INTO TINY PIECES.
YOUR BUDDY SIGN BINDING CONTRACT AND CONTRACT MUST ALWAYS BE HONORED.
YEAH?
WELL, MAYBE IT'S TIME WE RENEGOTIATED THE TERMS OF THAT CONTRACT, COMRADE.

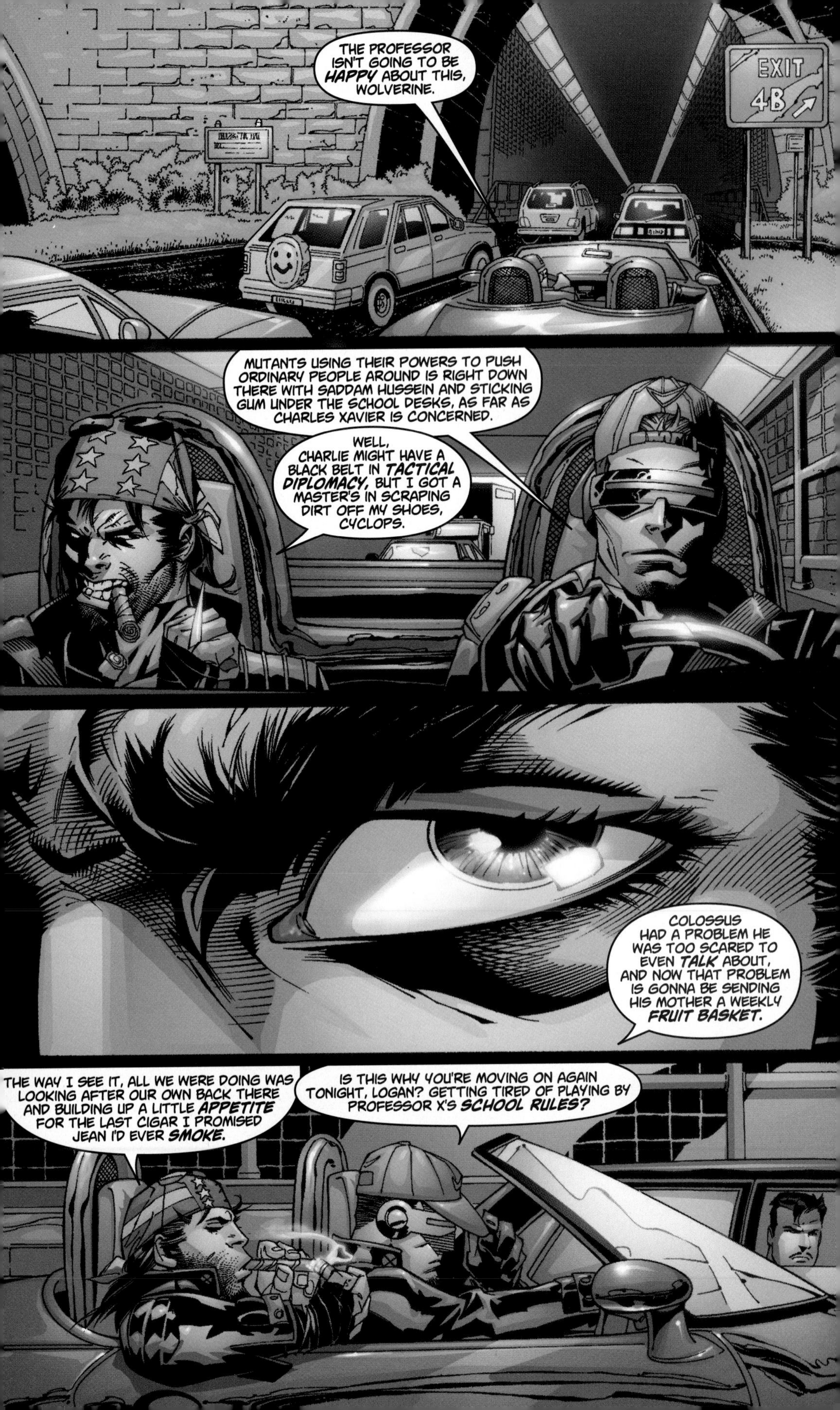

EXIT 4B
THE PROFESSOR ISN'T GOING TO BE HAPPY ABOUT THIS, WOLVERINE.
MUTANTS USING THEIR POWERS TO PUSH ORDINARY PEOPLE AROUND IS RIGHT DOWN THERE WITH SADDAM HUSSEIN AND STICKING GUM UNDER THE SCHOOL DESKS, AS FAR AS CHARLES XAVIER IS CONCERNED.
WELL, CHARLIE MIGHT HAVE A BLACK BELT IN TACTICAL DIPLOMACY, BUT I GOT A MASTER'S IN SCRAPING DIRT OFF MY SHOES, CYCLOPS.
COLOSSUS HAD A PROBLEM HE WAS TOO SCARED TO EVEN TALK ABOUT, AND NOW THAT PROBLEM IS GONNA BE SENDING HIS MOTHER A WEEKLY FRUIT BASKET.
THE WAY I SEE IT, ALL WE WERE DOING WAS LOOKING AFTER OUR OWN BACK THERE AND BUILDING UP A LITTLE APPETITE FOR THE LAST CIGAR I PROMISED JEAN I'D EVER SMOKE.
IS THIS WHY YOU'RE MOVING ON AGAIN TONIGHT, LOGAN? GETTING TIRED OF PLAYING BY PROFESSOR X'S SCHOOL RULES?

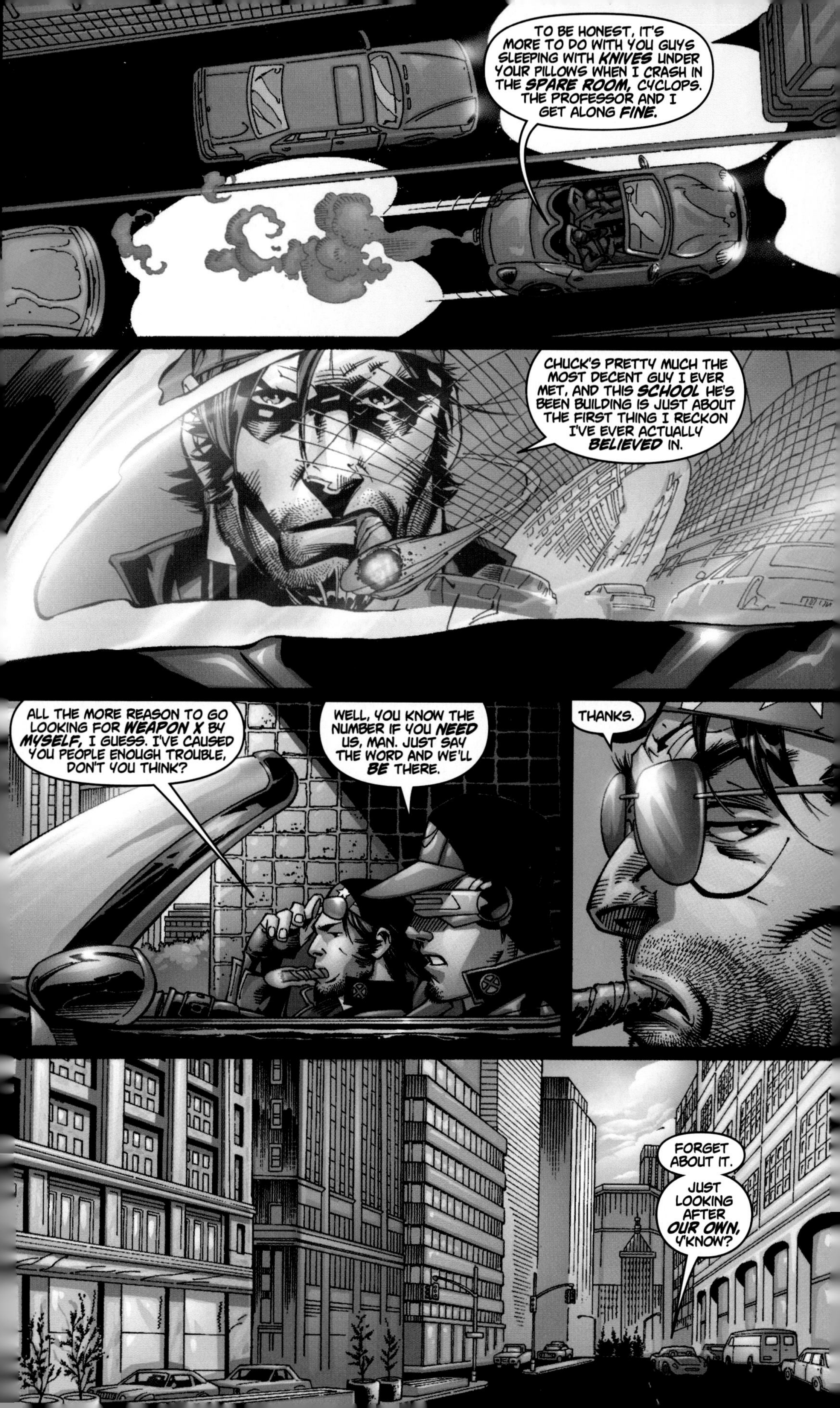
TO BE HONEST, IT'S MORE TO DO WITH YOU GUYS SLEEPING WITH KNIVES UNDER YOUR PILLOWS WHEN I CRASH IN THE SPARE ROOM, CYCLOPS. THE PROFESSOR AND I GET ALONG FINE.
CHUCK'S PRETTY MUCH THE MOST DECENT GUY I EVER MET, AND THIS SCHOOL HE'S BEEN BUILDING IS JUST ABOUT THE FIRST THING I RECKON I'VE EVER ACTUALLY BELIEVED IN.
ALL THE MORE REASON TO GO LOOKING FOR WEAPON X BY MYSELF, I GUESS. I'VE CAUSED YOU PEOPLE ENOUGH TROUBLE, DON'T YOU THINK?
WELL, YOU KNOW THE NUMBER IF YOU NEED US, MAN. JUST SAY THE WORD AND WE'LL BE THERE.
THANKS.
FORGET ABOUT IT.
JUST LOOKING AFTER OUR OWN, Y'KNOW?

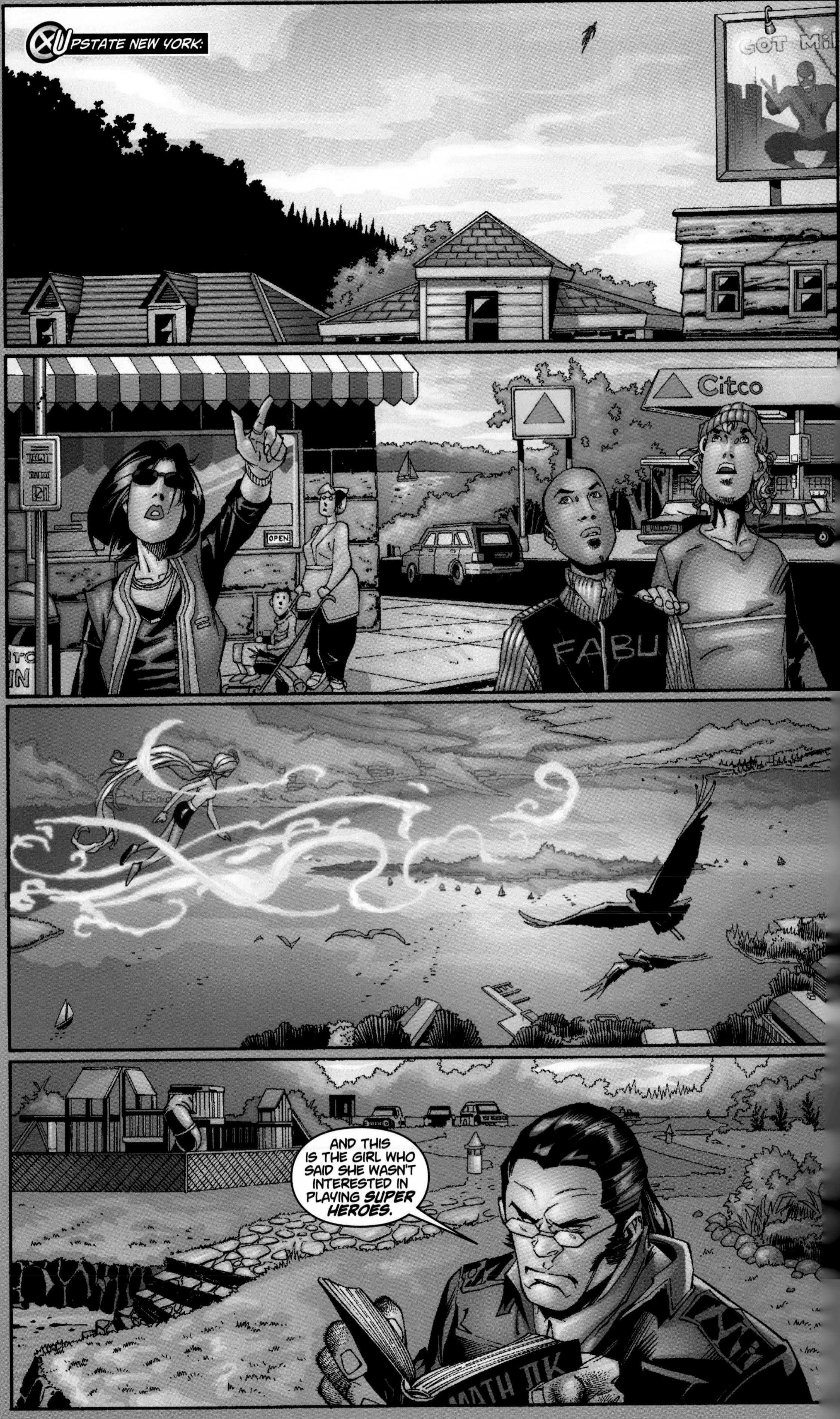
UPSTATE NEW YORK:
GOT MI
Citco
OPEN
FABU
AND THIS IS THE GIRL WHO SAID SHE WASN'T INTERESTED IN PLAYING *SUPER HEROES.*
MATH IIK

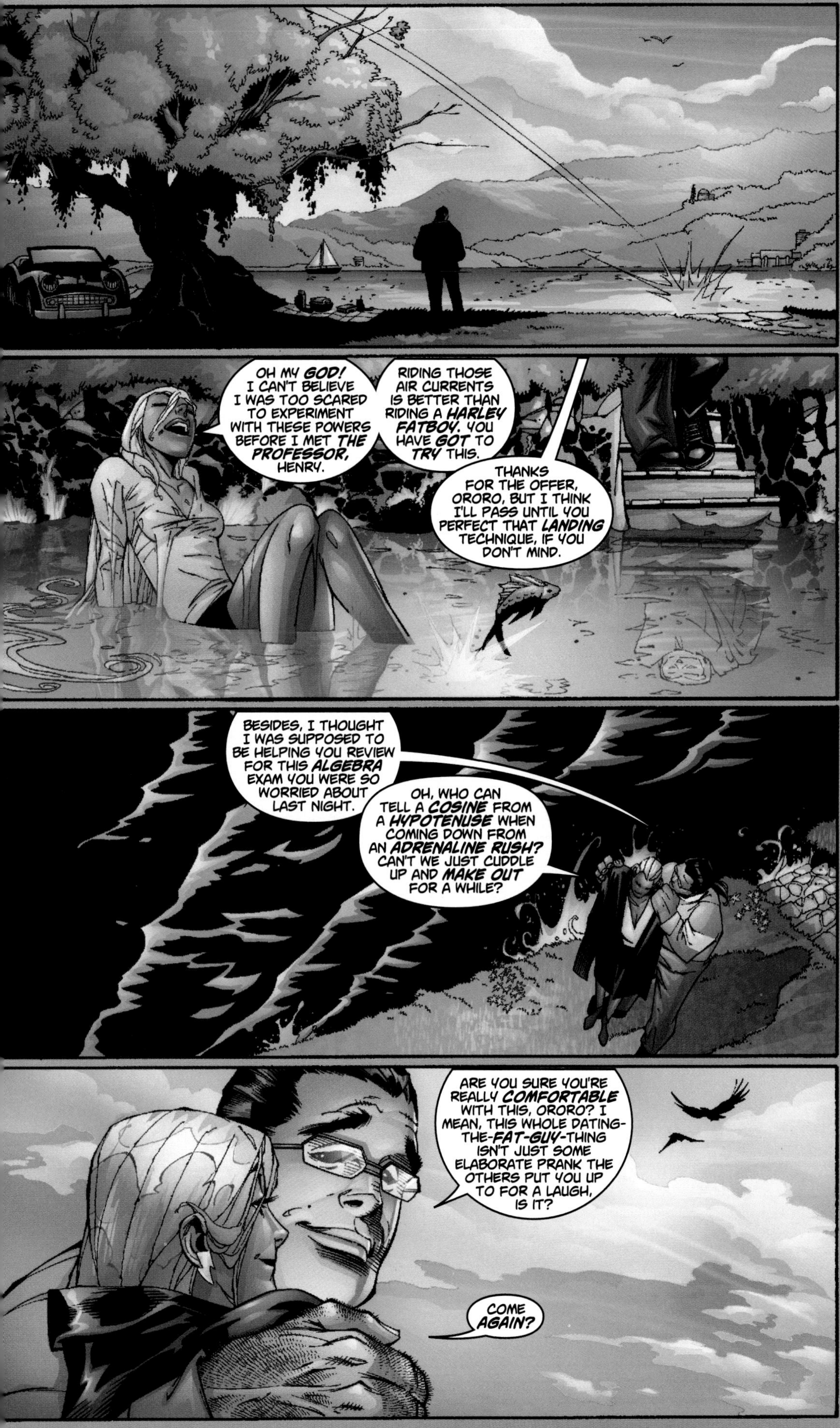
OH MY GOD! I CAN'T BELIEVE I WAS TOO SCARED TO EXPERIMENT WITH THESE POWERS BEFORE I MET THE PROFESSOR, HENRY.
RIDING THOSE AIR CURRENTS IS BETTER THAN RIDING A HARLEY FATBOY. YOU HAVE GOT TO TRY THIS.
THANKS FOR THE OFFER, ORORO, BUT I THINK I'LL PASS UNTIL YOU PERFECT THAT LANDING TECHNIQUE, IF YOU DON'T MIND.
BESIDES, I THOUGHT I WAS SUPPOSED TO BE HELPING YOU REVIEW FOR THIS ALGEBRA EXAM YOU WERE SO WORRIED ABOUT LAST NIGHT.
OH, WHO CAN TELL A COSINE FROM A HYPOTENUSE WHEN COMING DOWN FROM AN ADRENALINE RUSH? CAN'T WE JUST CUDDLE UP AND MAKE OUT FOR A WHILE?
ARE YOU SURE YOU'RE REALLY COMFORTABLE WITH THIS, ORORO? I MEAN, THIS WHOLE DATING-THE-FAT-GUY-THING ISN'T JUST SOME ELABORATE PRANK THE OTHERS PUT YOU UP TO FOR A LAUGH, IS IT?
COME AGAIN?

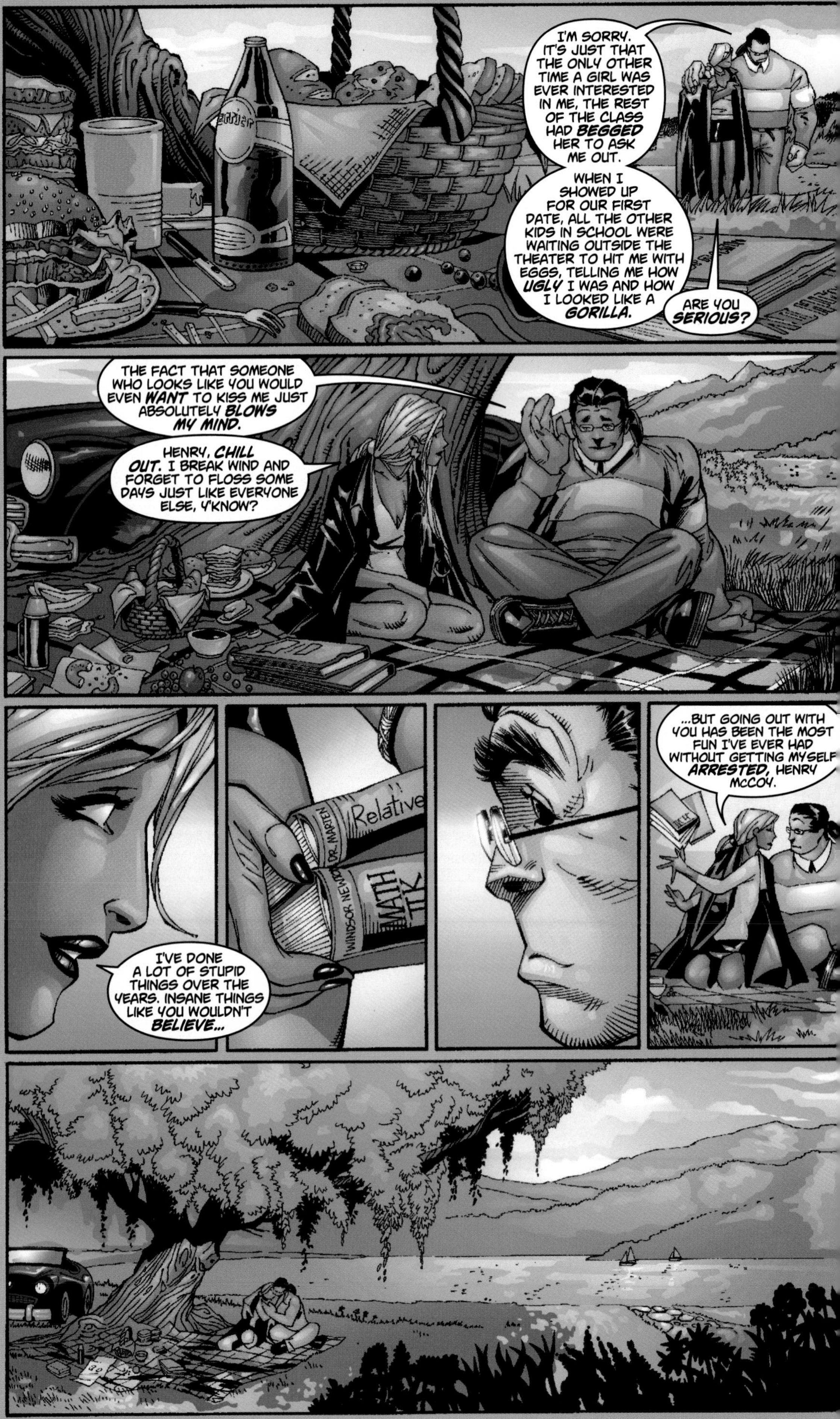
I'M SORRY. IT'S JUST THAT THE ONLY OTHER TIME A GIRL WAS EVER INTERESTED IN ME, THE REST OF THE CLASS HAD BEGGED HER TO ASK ME OUT.
WHEN I SHOWED UP FOR OUR FIRST DATE, ALL THE OTHER KIDS IN SCHOOL WERE WAITING OUTSIDE THE THEATER TO HIT ME WITH EGGS, TELLING ME HOW UGLY I WAS AND HOW I LOOKED LIKE A GORILLA.
ARE YOU SERIOUS?
THE FACT THAT SOMEONE WHO LOOKS LIKE YOU WOULD EVEN WANT TO KISS ME JUST ABSOLUTELY BLOWS MY MIND.
HENRY, CHILL OUT. I BREAK WIND AND FORGET TO FLOSS SOME DAYS JUST LIKE EVERYONE ELSE, Y'KNOW?
I'VE DONE A LOT OF STUPID THINGS OVER THE YEARS. INSANE THINGS LIKE YOU WOULDN'T BELIEVE...
Relative
DR. MARTEN
WINDSOR NEWTON
MATH
...BUT GOING OUT WITH YOU HAS BEEN THE MOST FUN I'VE EVER HAD WITHOUT GETTING MYSELF ARRESTED, HENRY McCOY.

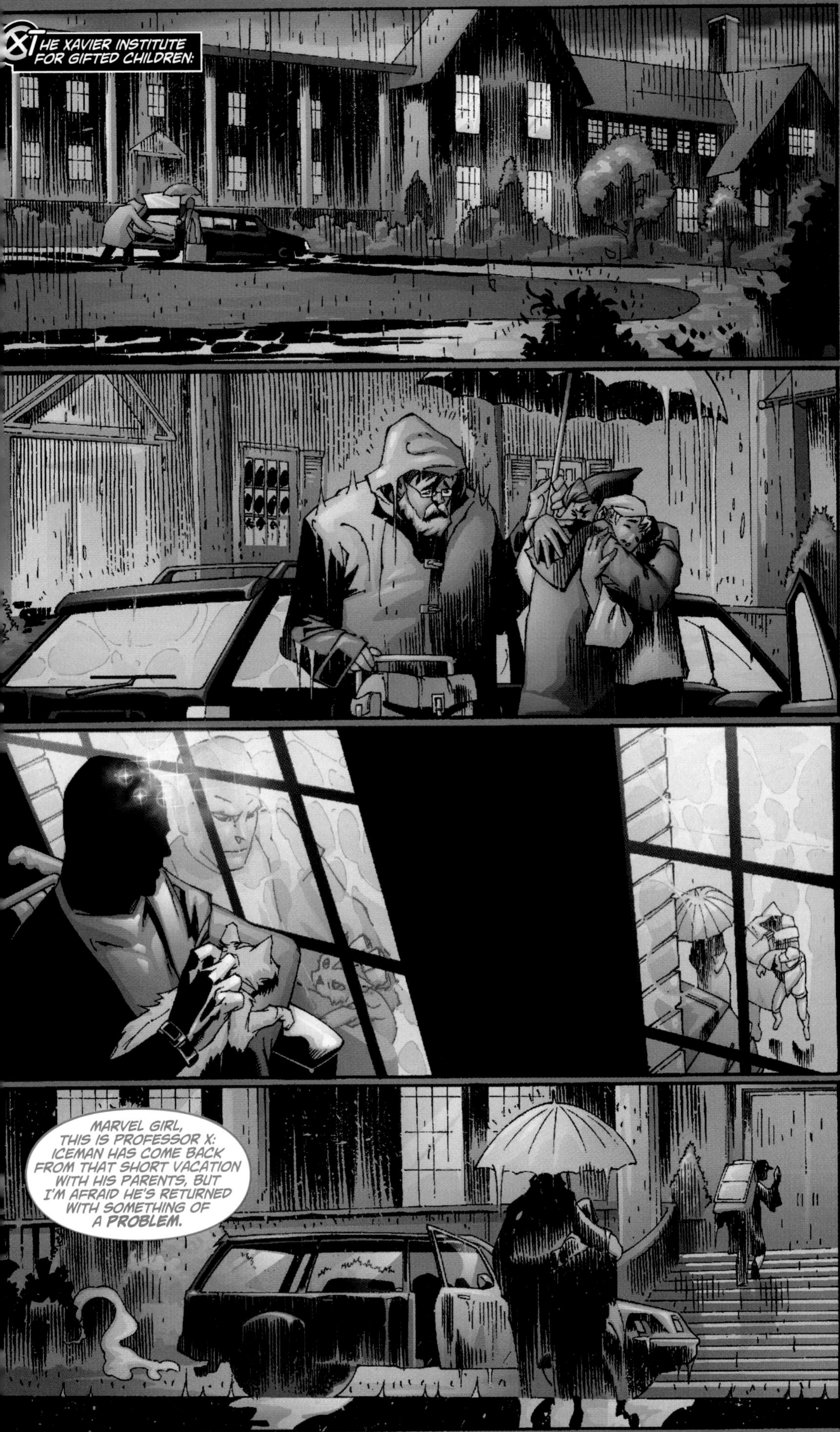
THE XAVIER INSTITUTE FOR GIFTED CHILDREN:
MARVEL GIRL, THIS IS PROFESSOR X: ICEMAN HAS COME BACK FROM THAT SHORT VACATION WITH HIS PARENTS, BUT I'M AFRAID HE'S RETURNED WITH SOMETHING OF A PROBLEM.

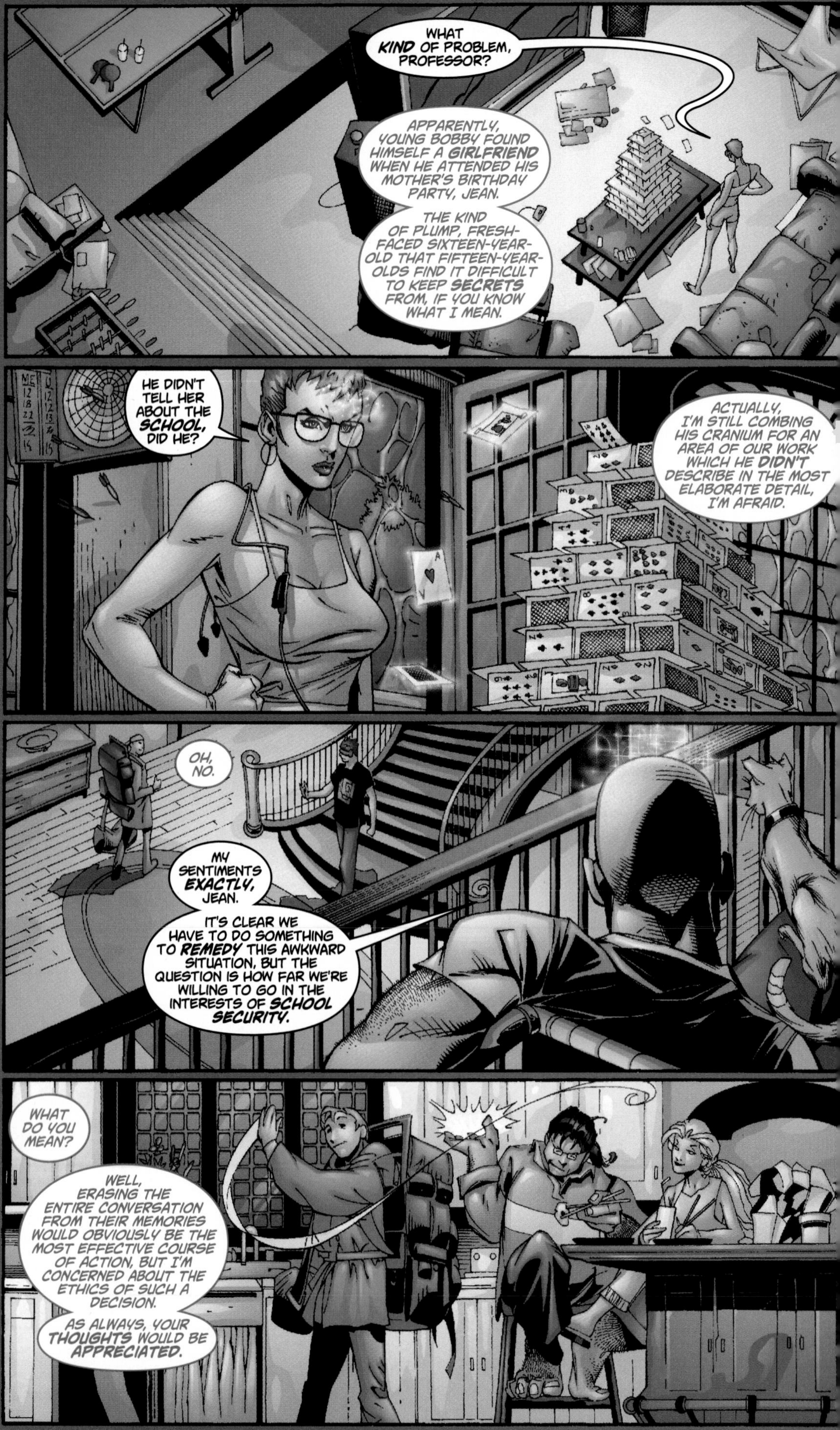
WHAT KIND OF PROBLEM, PROFESSOR?
APPARENTLY, YOUNG BOBBY FOUND HIMSELF A GIRLFRIEND WHEN HE ATTENDED HIS MOTHER'S BIRTHDAY PARTY, JEAN.
THE KIND OF PLUMP, FRESH-FACED SIXTEEN-YEAR-OLD THAT FIFTEEN-YEAR-OLDS FIND IT DIFFICULT TO KEEP SECRETS FROM, IF YOU KNOW WHAT I MEAN.
HE DIDN'T TELL HER ABOUT THE SCHOOL, DID HE?
ACTUALLY, I'M STILL COMBING HIS CRANIUM FOR AN AREA OF OUR WORK WHICH HE DIDN'T DESCRIBE IN THE MOST ELABORATE DETAIL, I'M AFRAID.
OH, NO.
MY SENTIMENTS EXACTLY, JEAN.
IT'S CLEAR WE HAVE TO DO SOMETHING TO REMEDY THIS AWKWARD SITUATION, BUT THE QUESTION IS HOW FAR WE'RE WILLING TO GO IN THE INTERESTS OF SCHOOL SECURITY.
WHAT DO YOU MEAN?
WELL, ERASING THE ENTIRE CONVERSATION FROM THEIR MEMORIES WOULD OBVIOUSLY BE THE MOST EFFECTIVE COURSE OF ACTION, BUT I'M CONCERNED ABOUT THE ETHICS OF SUCH A DECISION.
AS ALWAYS, YOUR THOUGHTS WOULD BE APPRECIATED.

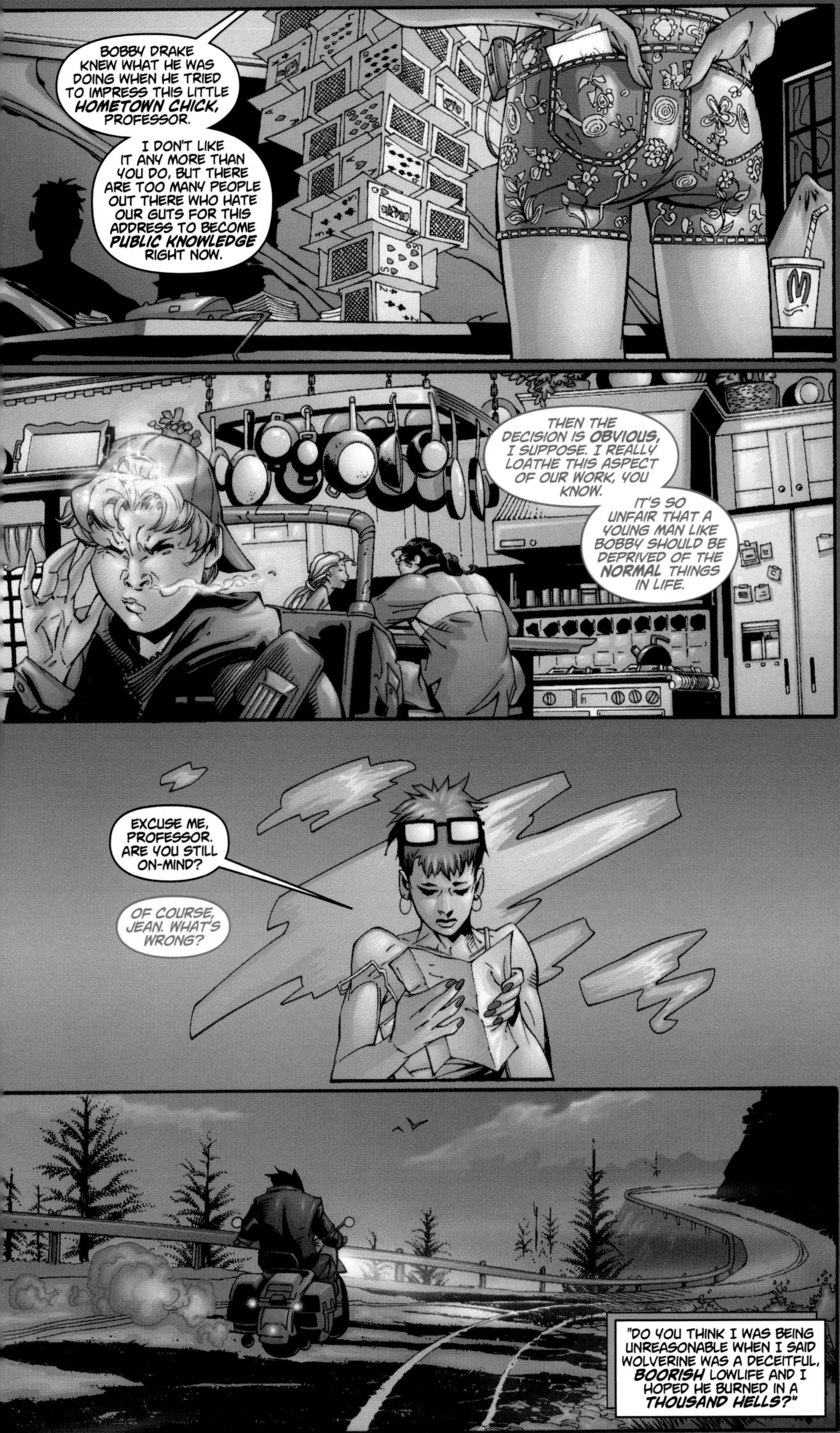
BOBBY DRAKE KNEW WHAT HE WAS DOING WHEN HE TRIED TO IMPRESS THIS LITTLE HOMETOWN CHICK, PROFESSOR.
I DON'T LIKE IT ANY MORE THAN YOU DO, BUT THERE ARE TOO MANY PEOPLE OUT THERE WHO HATE OUR GUTS FOR THIS ADDRESS TO BECOME PUBLIC KNOWLEDGE RIGHT NOW.
THEN THE DECISION IS OBVIOUS, I SUPPOSE. I REALLY LOATHE THIS ASPECT OF OUR WORK, YOU KNOW.
IT'S SO UNFAIR THAT A YOUNG MAN LIKE BOBBY SHOULD BE DEPRIVED OF THE NORMAL THINGS IN LIFE.
EXCUSE ME, PROFESSOR. ARE YOU STILL ON-MIND?
OF COURSE, JEAN. WHAT'S WRONG?
"DO YOU THINK I WAS BEING UNREASONABLE WHEN I SAID WOLVERINE WAS A DECEITFUL, BOORISH LOWLIFE AND I HOPED HE BURNED IN A THOUSAND HELLS?"

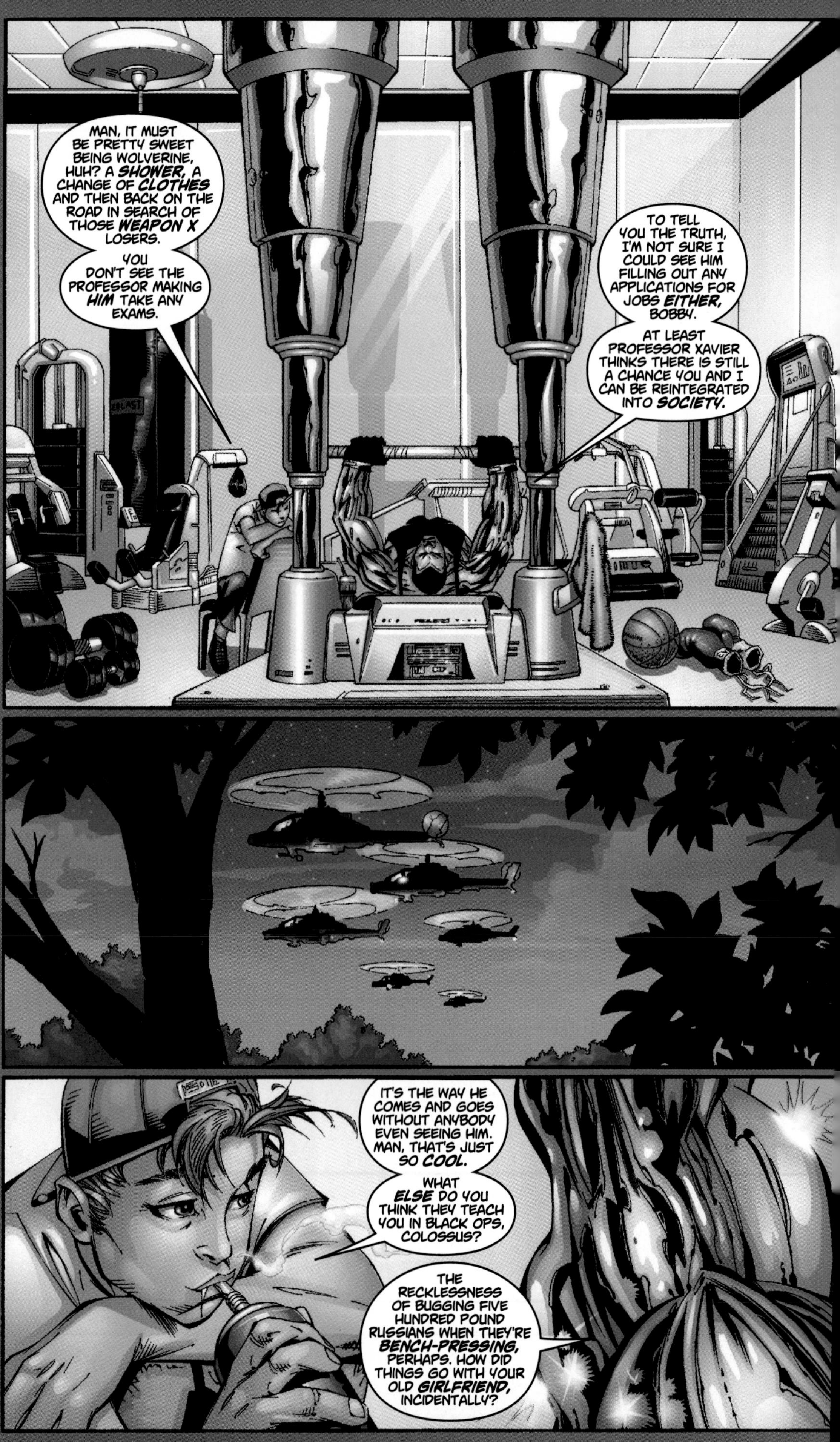
MAN, IT MUST BE PRETTY SWEET BEING WOLVERINE, HUH? A SHOWER, A CHANGE OF CLOTHES AND THEN BACK ON THE ROAD IN SEARCH OF THOSE WEAPON X LOSERS.
YOU DON'T SEE THE PROFESSOR MAKING HIM TAKE ANY EXAMS.
TO TELL YOU THE TRUTH, I'M NOT SURE I COULD SEE HIM FILLING OUT ANY APPLICATIONS FOR JOBS EITHER, BOBBY.
AT LEAST PROFESSOR XAVIER THINKS THERE IS STILL A CHANCE YOU AND I CAN BE REINTEGRATED INTO SOCIETY.
IT'S THE WAY HE COMES AND GOES WITHOUT ANYBODY EVEN SEEING HIM. MAN, THAT'S JUST SO COOL.
WHAT ELSE DO YOU THINK THEY TEACH YOU IN BLACK OPS, COLOSSUS?
THE RECKLESSNESS OF BUGGING FIVE HUNDRED POUND RUSSIANS WHEN THEY'RE BENCH-PRESSING, PERHAPS. HOW DID THINGS GO WITH YOUR OLD GIRLFRIEND, INCIDENTALLY?

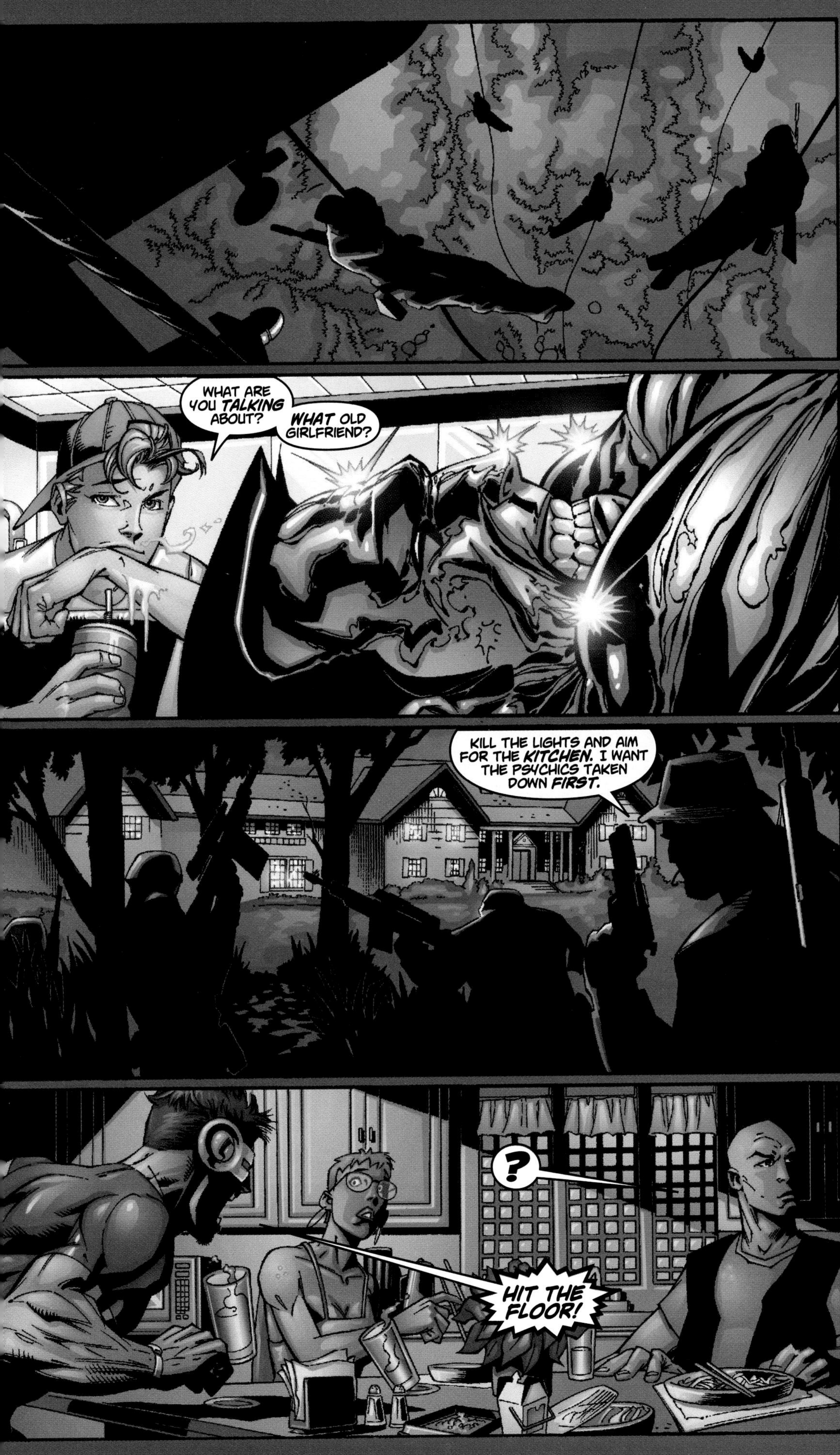
WHAT ARE YOU TALKING ABOUT?
WHAT OLD GIRLFRIEND?
KILL THE LIGHTS AND AIM FOR THE KITCHEN. I WANT THE PSYCHICS TAKEN DOWN FIRST.
?
HIT THE FLOOR!

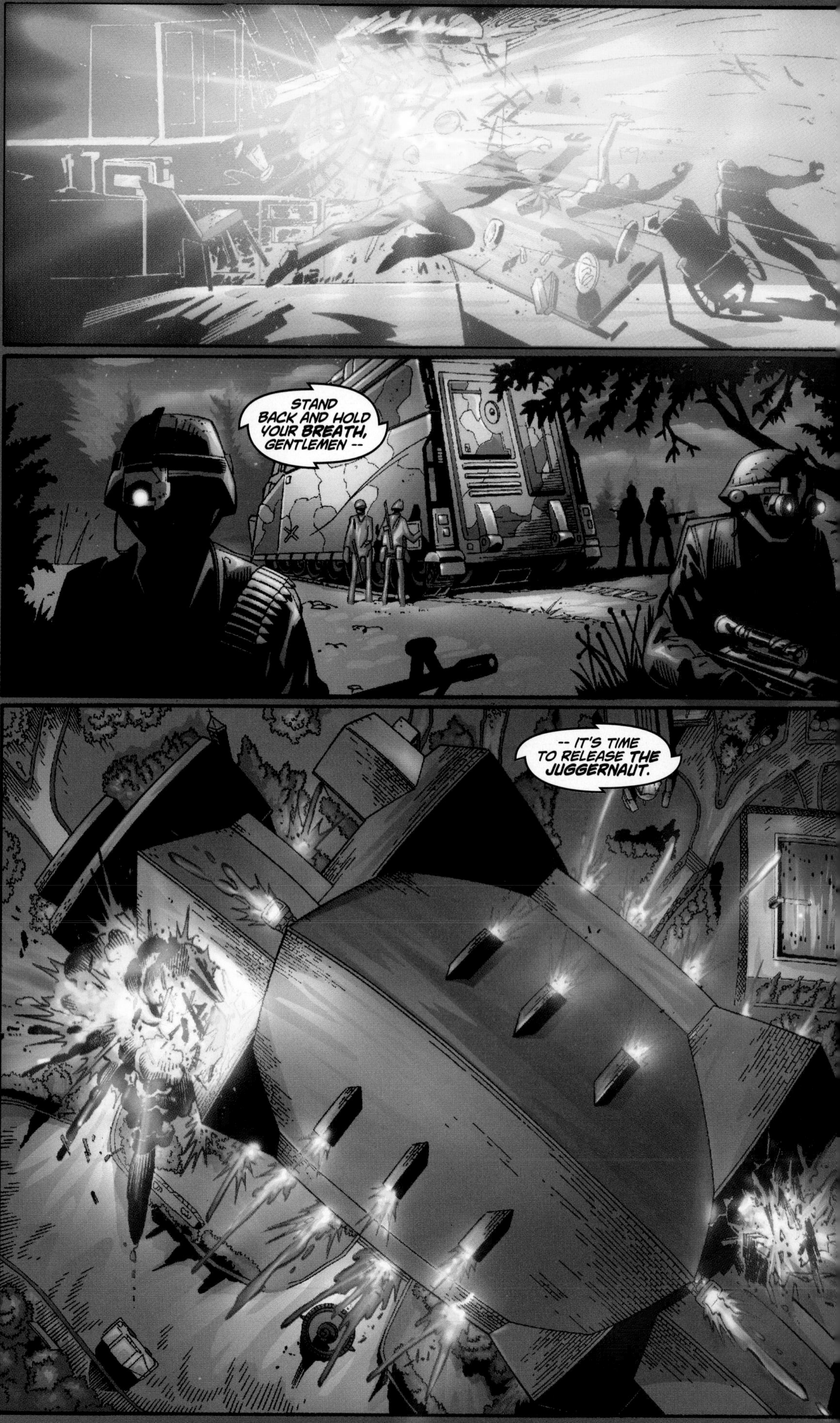
STAND BACK AND HOLD YOUR BREATH, GENTLEMEN --
-- IT'S TIME TO RELEASE THE JUGGERNAUT.

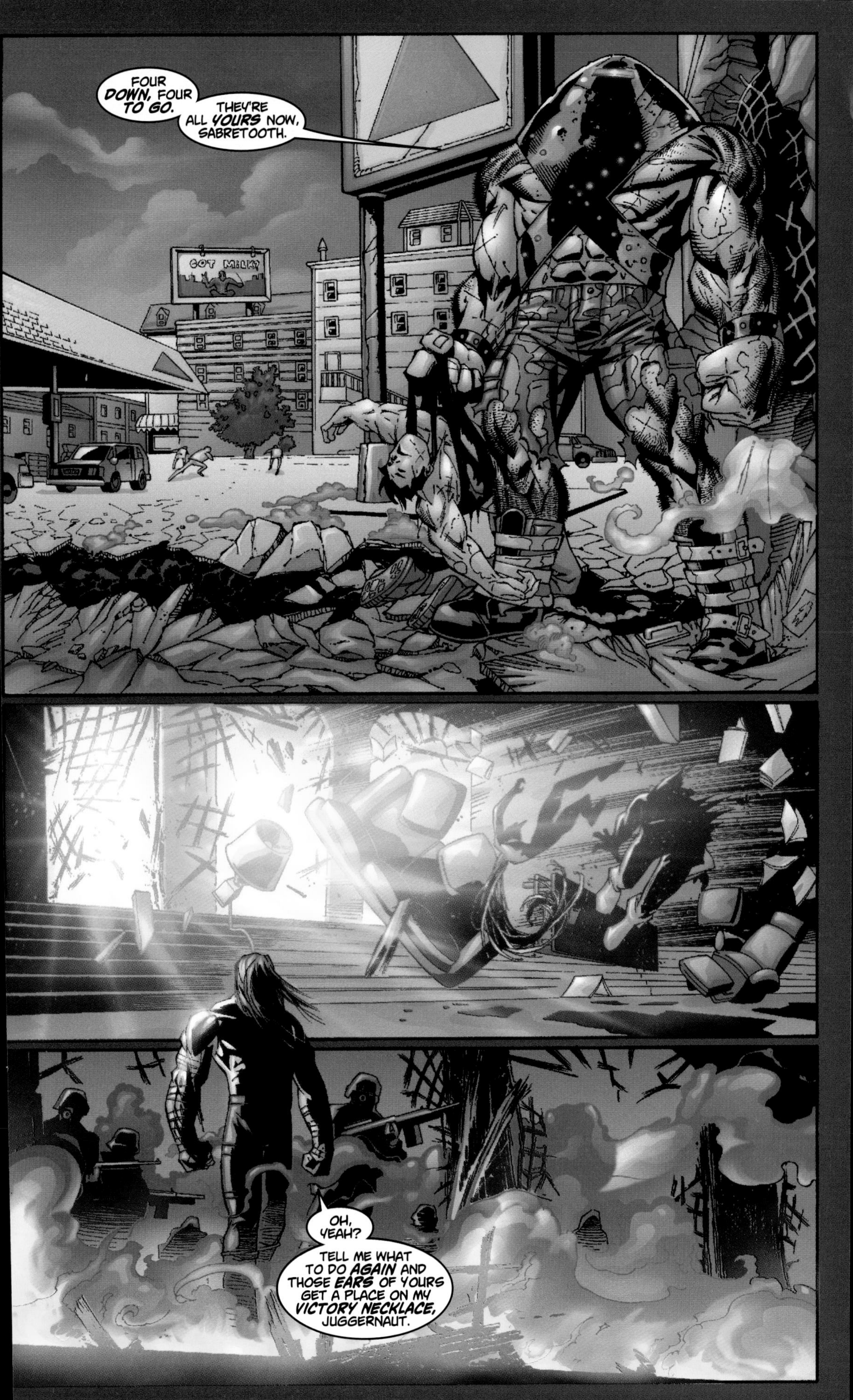
FOUR DOWN, FOUR TO GO.
THEY'RE ALL YOURS NOW, SABRETOOTH.
GOT MILK?
OH, YEAH?
TELL ME WHAT TO DO AGAIN AND THOSE EARS OF YOURS GET A PLACE ON MY VICTORY NECKLACE, JUGGERNAUT.

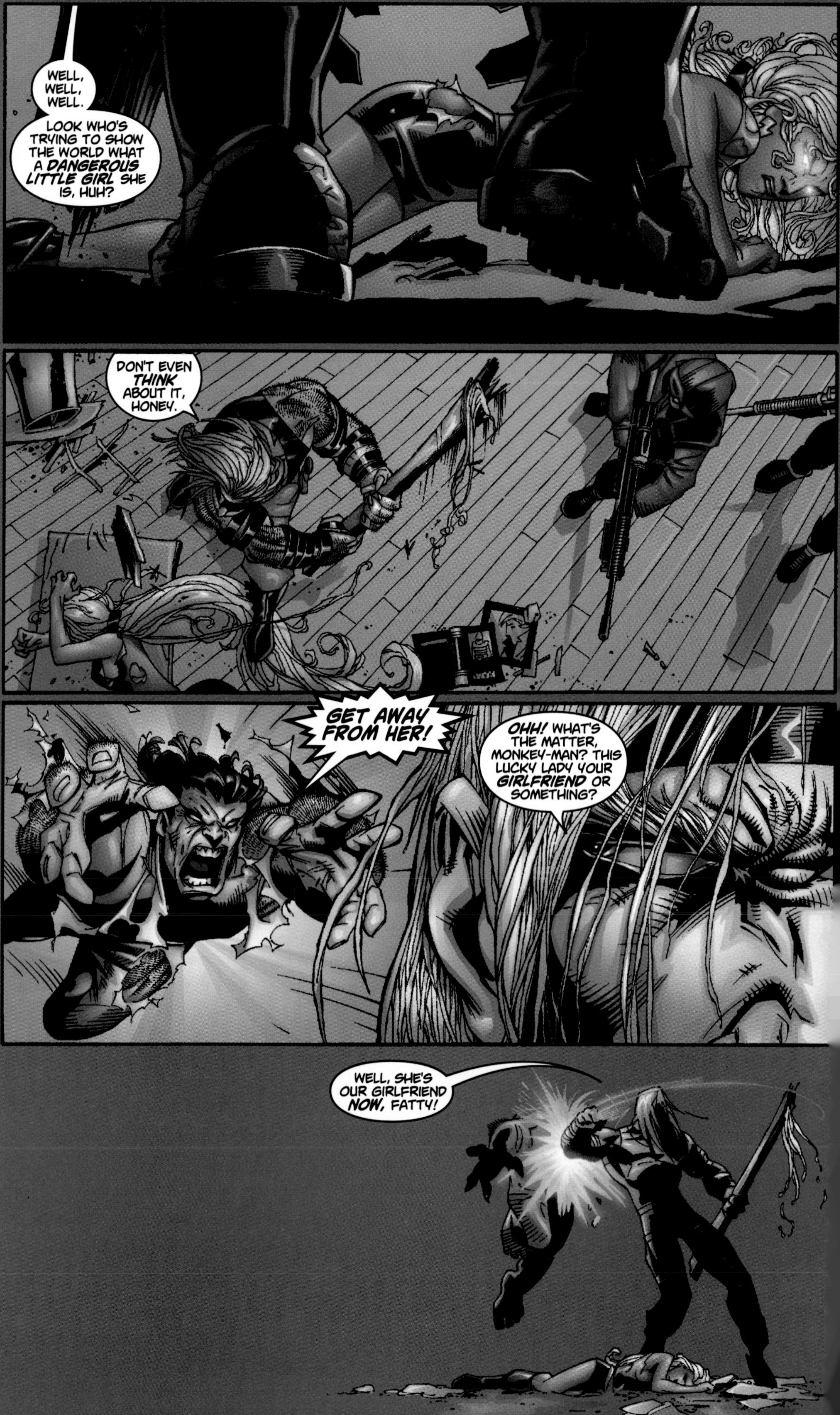
WELL, WELL, WELL.
LOOK WHO'S TRYING TO SHOW THE WORLD WHAT A DANGEROUS LITTLE GIRL SHE IS, HUH?
DON'T EVEN THINK ABOUT IT, HONEY.
GET AWAY FROM HER!
OHH! WHAT'S THE MATTER, MONKEY-MAN? THIS LUCKY LADY YOUR GIRLFRIEND OR SOMETHING?
WELL, SHE'S OUR GIRLFRIEND NOW, FATTY!

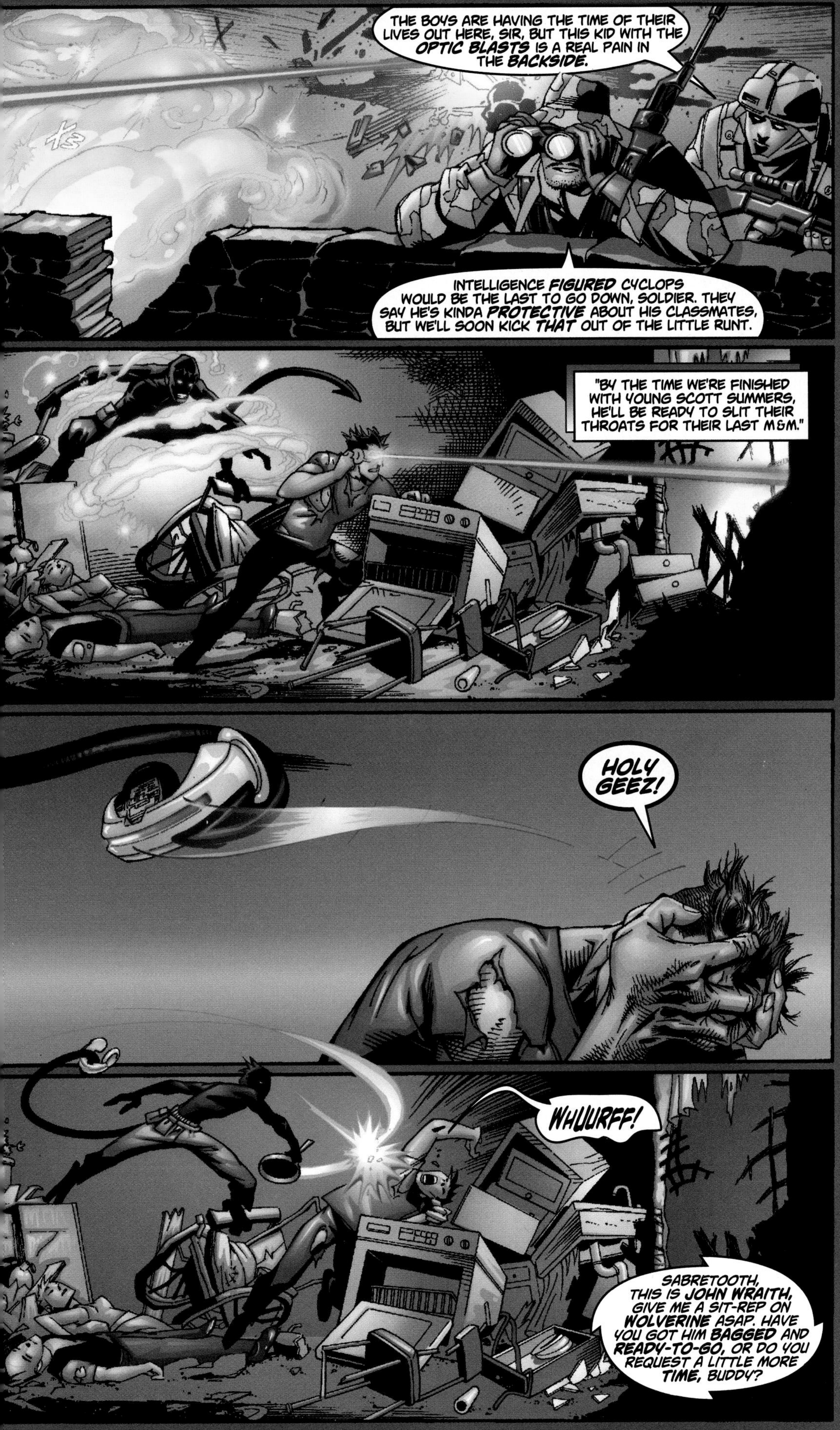
THE BOYS ARE HAVING THE TIME OF THEIR LIVES OUT HERE, SIR, BUT THIS KID WITH THE OPTIC BLASTS IS A REAL PAIN IN THE BACKSIDE.
INTELLIGENCE FIGURED CYCLOPS WOULD BE THE LAST TO GO DOWN, SOLDIER. THEY SAY HE'S KINDA PROTECTIVE ABOUT HIS CLASSMATES, BUT WE'LL SOON KICK THAT OUT OF THE LITTLE RUNT.
"BY THE TIME WE'RE FINISHED WITH YOUNG SCOTT SUMMERS, HE'LL BE READY TO SLIT THEIR THROATS FOR THEIR LAST M&M."
HOLY GEEZ!
WHUURFF!
SABRETOOTH, THIS IS JOHN WRAITH, GIVE ME A SIT-REP ON WOLVERINE ASAP. HAVE YOU GOT HIM BAGGED AND READY-TO-GO, OR DO YOU REQUEST A LITTLE MORE TIME, BUDDY?

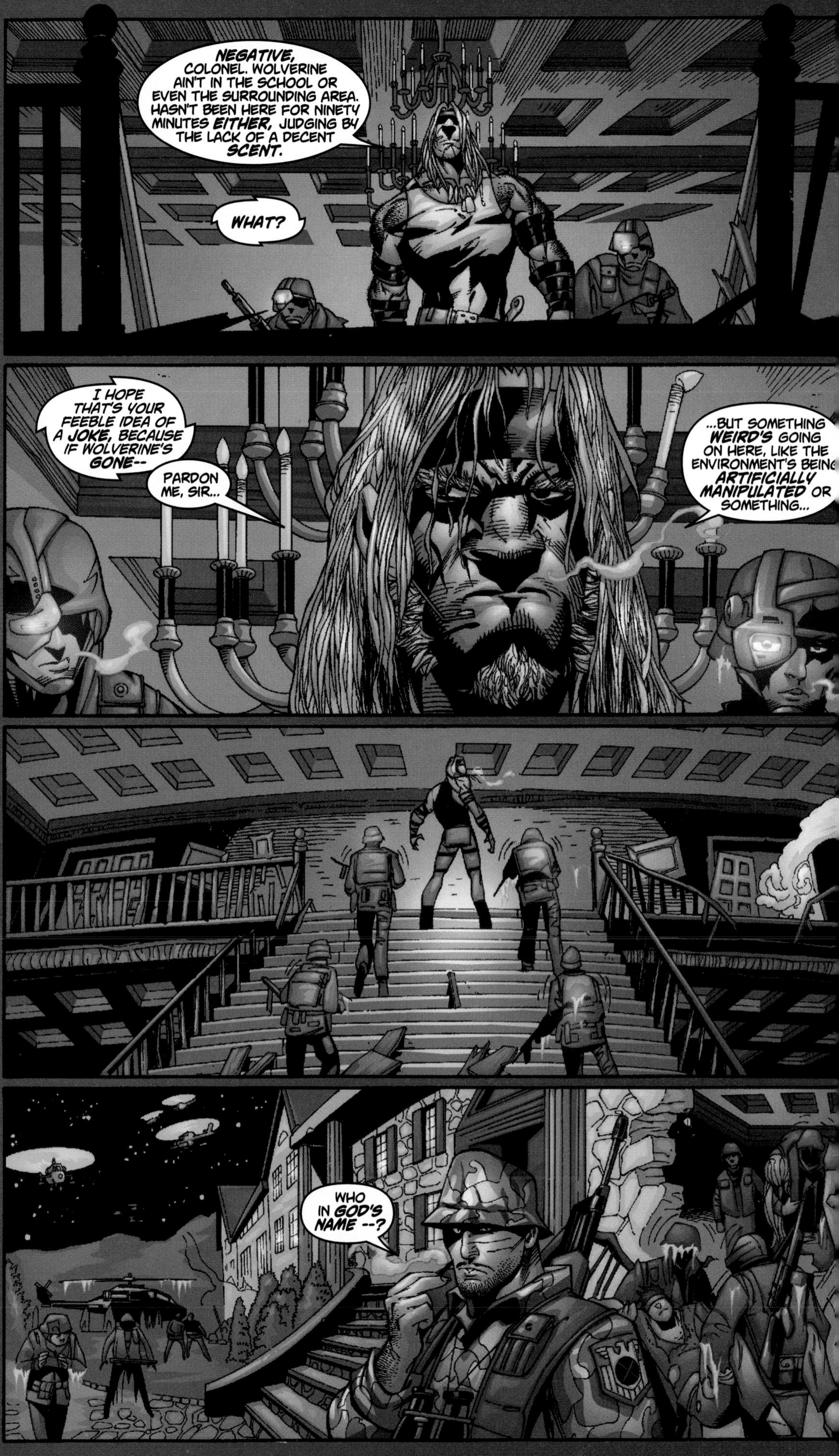
NEGATIVE, COLONEL. WOLVERINE AIN'T IN THE SCHOOL OR EVEN THE SURROUNDING AREA. HASN'T BEEN HERE FOR NINETY MINUTES EITHER, JUDGING BY THE LACK OF A DECENT SCENT.
WHAT?
I HOPE THAT'S YOUR FEEBLE IDEA OF A JOKE, BECAUSE IF WOLVERINE'S GONE--
PARDON ME, SIR...
...BUT SOMETHING WEIRD'S GOING ON HERE, LIKE THE ENVIRONMENT'S BEING ARTIFICIALLY MANIPULATED OR SOMETHING...
WHO IN GOD'S NAME --?

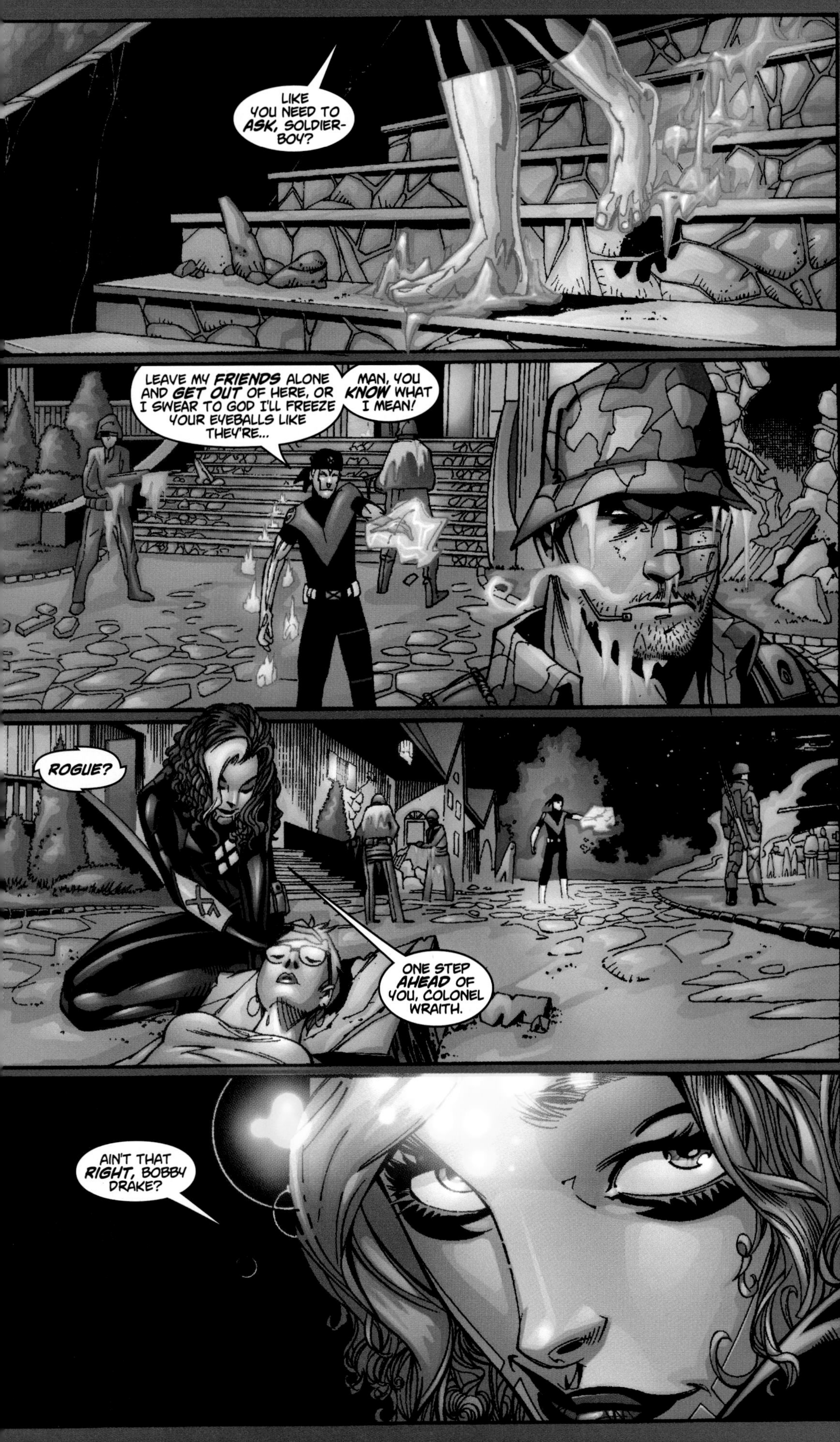
LIKE YOU NEED TO ASK, SOLDIER-BOY?
LEAVE MY FRIENDS ALONE AND GET OUT OF HERE, OR I SWEAR TO GOD I'LL FREEZE YOUR EYEBALLS LIKE THEY'RE...
MAN, YOU KNOW WHAT I MEAN!
ROGUE?
ONE STEP AHEAD OF YOU, COLONEL WRAITH.
AIN'T THAT RIGHT, BOBBY DRAKE?

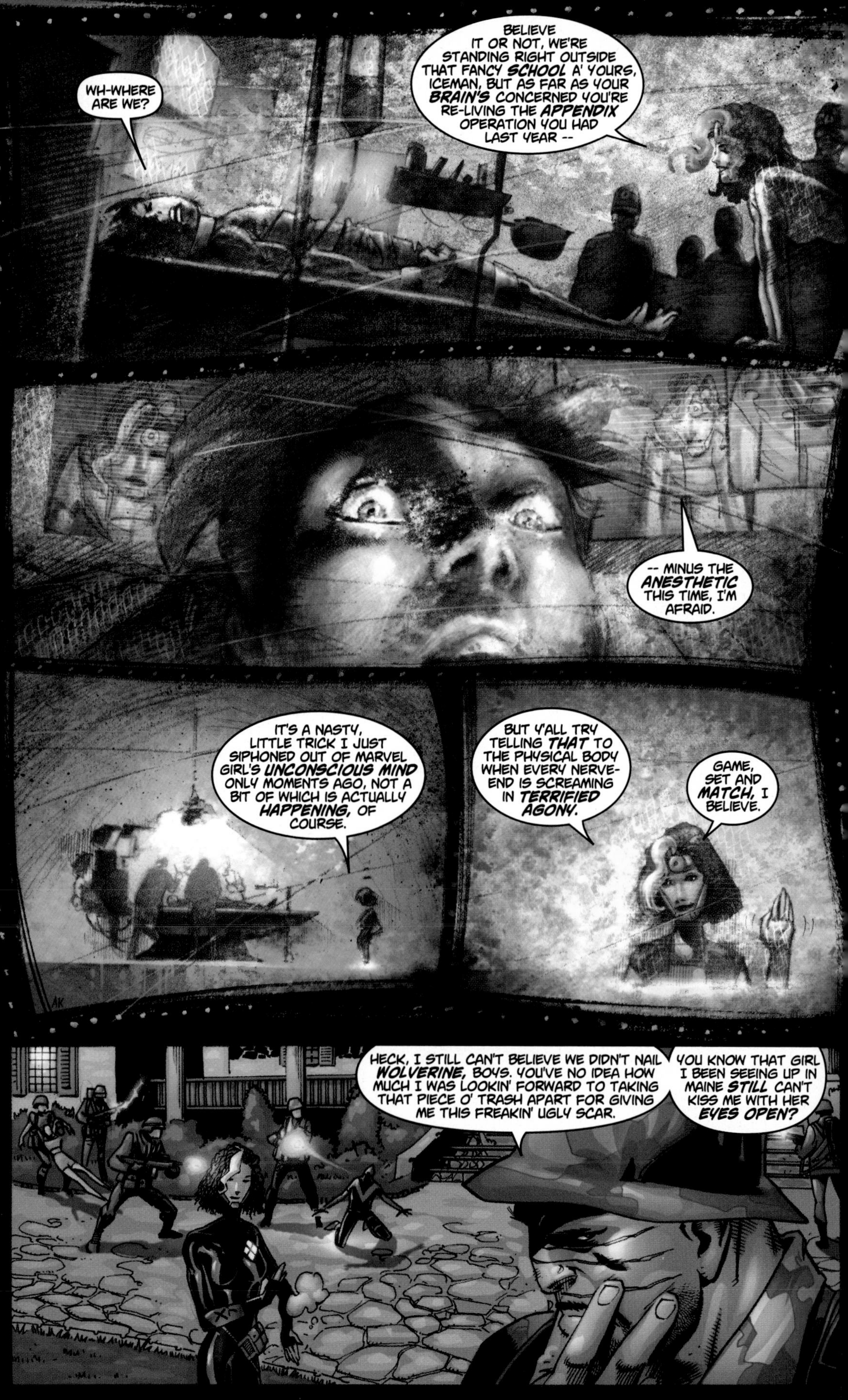
WH-WHERE ARE WE?
BELIEVE IT OR NOT, WE'RE STANDING RIGHT OUTSIDE THAT FANCY SCHOOL A' YOURS, ICEMAN, BUT AS FAR AS YOUR BRAIN'S CONCERNED YOU'RE RE-LIVING THE APPENDIX OPERATION YOU HAD LAST YEAR --
-- MINUS THE ANESTHETIC THIS TIME, I'M AFRAID.
IT'S A NASTY, LITTLE TRICK I JUST SIPHONED OUT OF MARVEL GIRL'S UNCONSCIOUS MIND ONLY MOMENTS AGO, NOT A BIT OF WHICH IS ACTUALLY HAPPENING, OF COURSE.
BUT Y'ALL TRY TELLING THAT TO THE PHYSICAL BODY WHEN EVERY NERVE-END IS SCREAMING IN TERRIFIED AGONY.
GAME, SET AND MATCH, I BELIEVE.
AK
HECK, I STILL CAN'T BELIEVE WE DIDN'T NAIL WOLVERINE, BOYS. YOU'VE NO IDEA HOW MUCH I WAS LOOKIN' FORWARD TO TAKING THAT PIECE O' TRASH APART FOR GIVING ME THIS FREAKIN' UGLY SCAR.
YOU KNOW THAT GIRL I BEEN SEEING UP IN MAINE STILL CAN'T KISS ME WITH HER EYES OPEN?

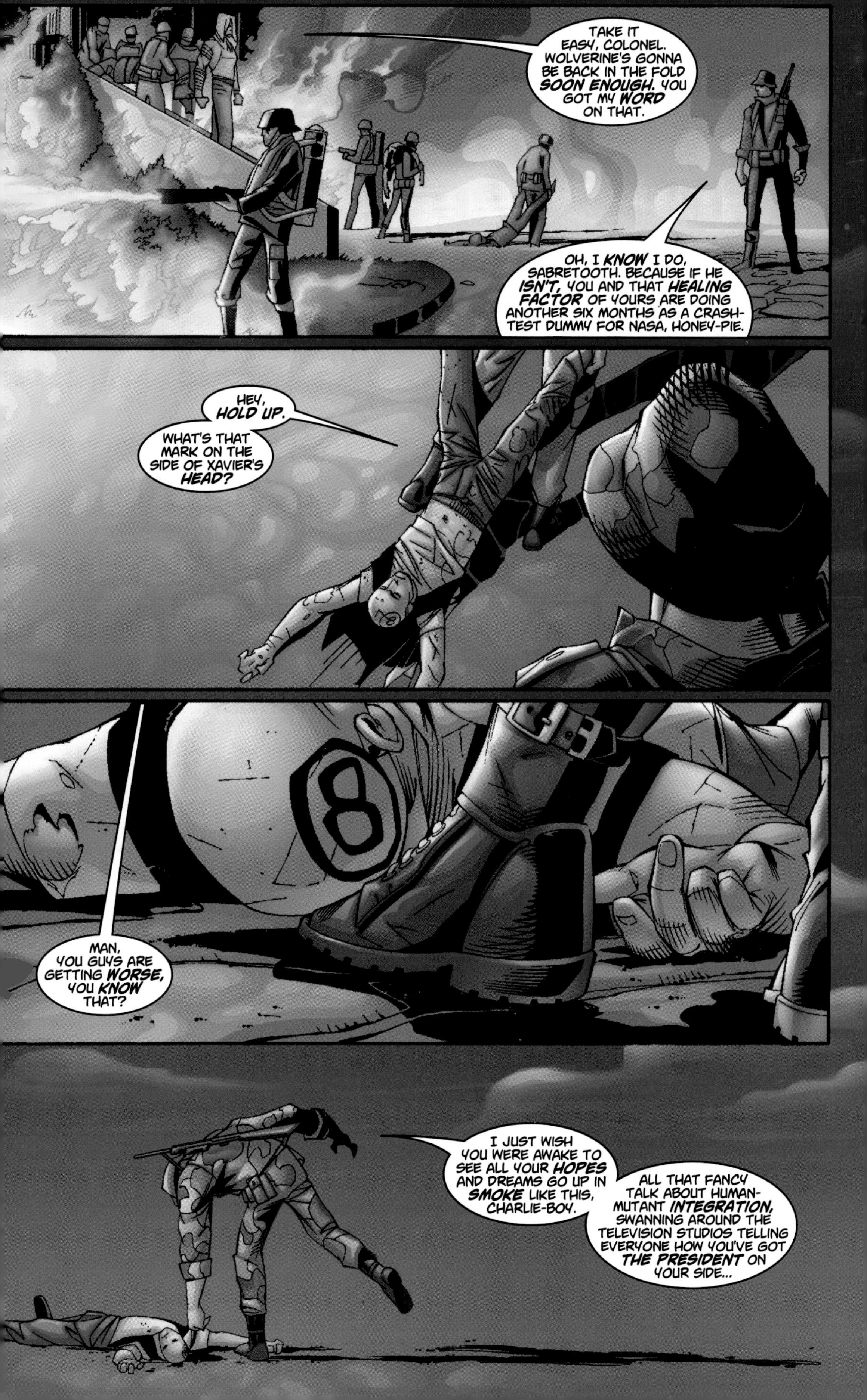
TAKE IT EASY, COLONEL. WOLVERINE'S GONNA BE BACK IN THE FOLD SOON ENOUGH. YOU GOT MY WORD ON THAT.
OH, I KNOW I DO, SABRETOOTH. BECAUSE IF HE ISN'T, YOU AND THAT HEALING FACTOR OF YOURS ARE DOING ANOTHER SIX MONTHS AS A CRASH-TEST DUMMY FOR NASA, HONEY-PIE.
HEY, HOLD UP.
WHAT'S THAT MARK ON THE SIDE OF XAVIER'S HEAD?
MAN, YOU GUYS ARE GETTING WORSE, YOU KNOW THAT?
I JUST WISH YOU WERE AWAKE TO SEE ALL YOUR HOPES AND DREAMS GO UP IN SMOKE LIKE THIS, CHARLIE-BOY.
ALL THAT FANCY TALK ABOUT HUMAN-MUTANT INTEGRATION, SWANNING AROUND THE TELEVISION STUDIOS TELLING EVERYONE HOW YOU'VE GOT THE PRESIDENT ON YOUR SIDE...

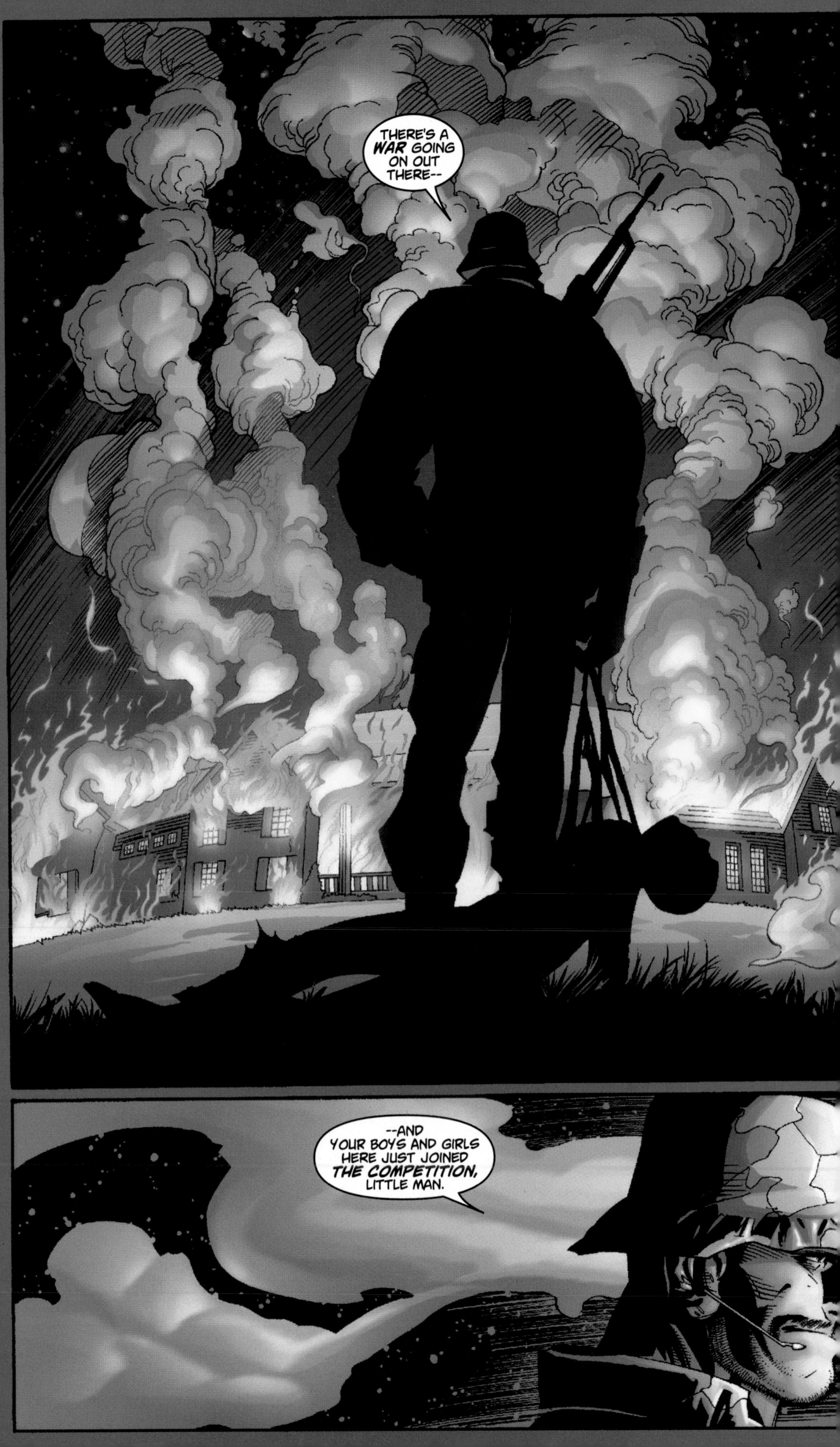
THERE'S A WAR GOING ON OUT THERE--
--AND YOUR BOYS AND GIRLS HERE JUST JOINED THE COMPETITION, LITTLE MAN.

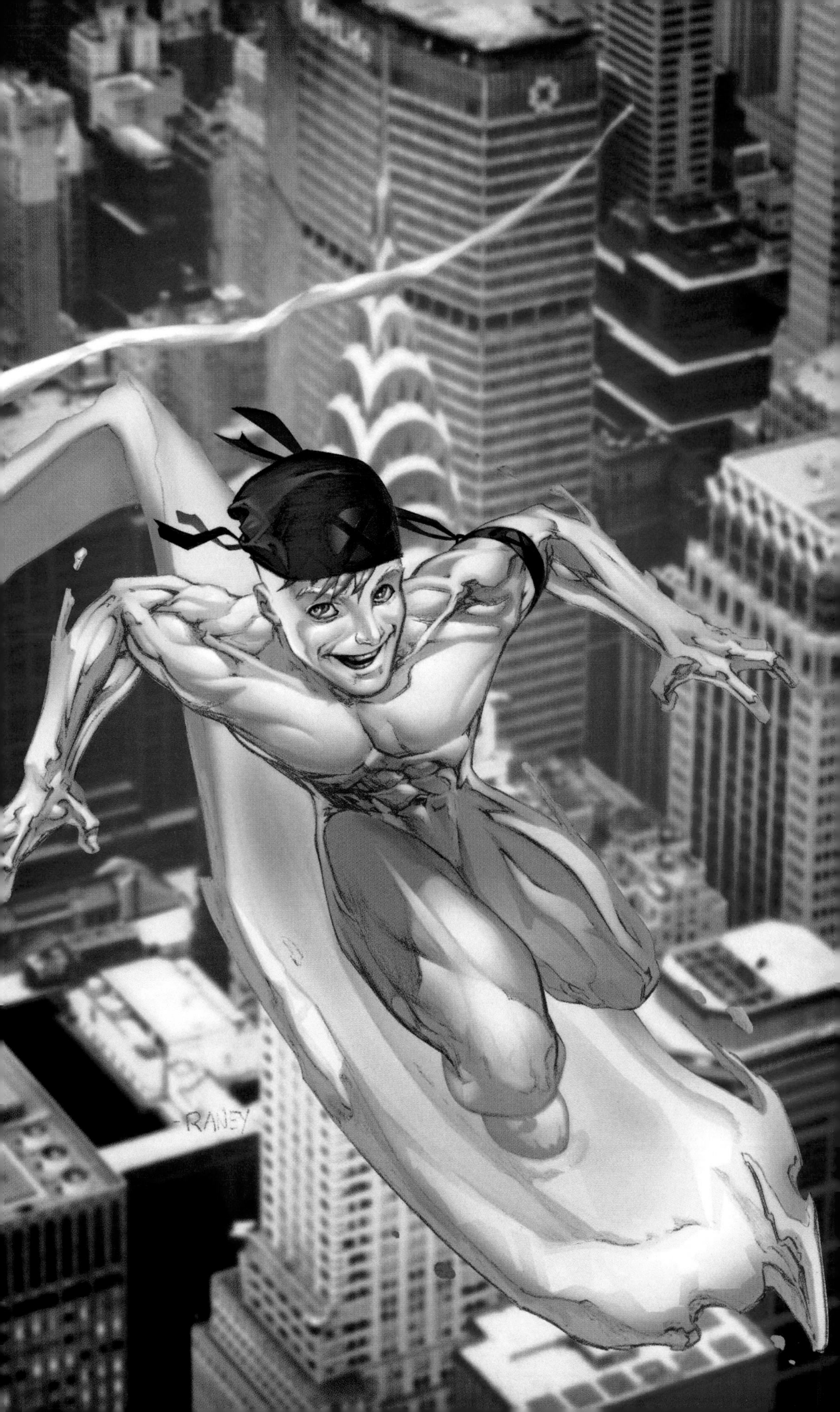
RANEY

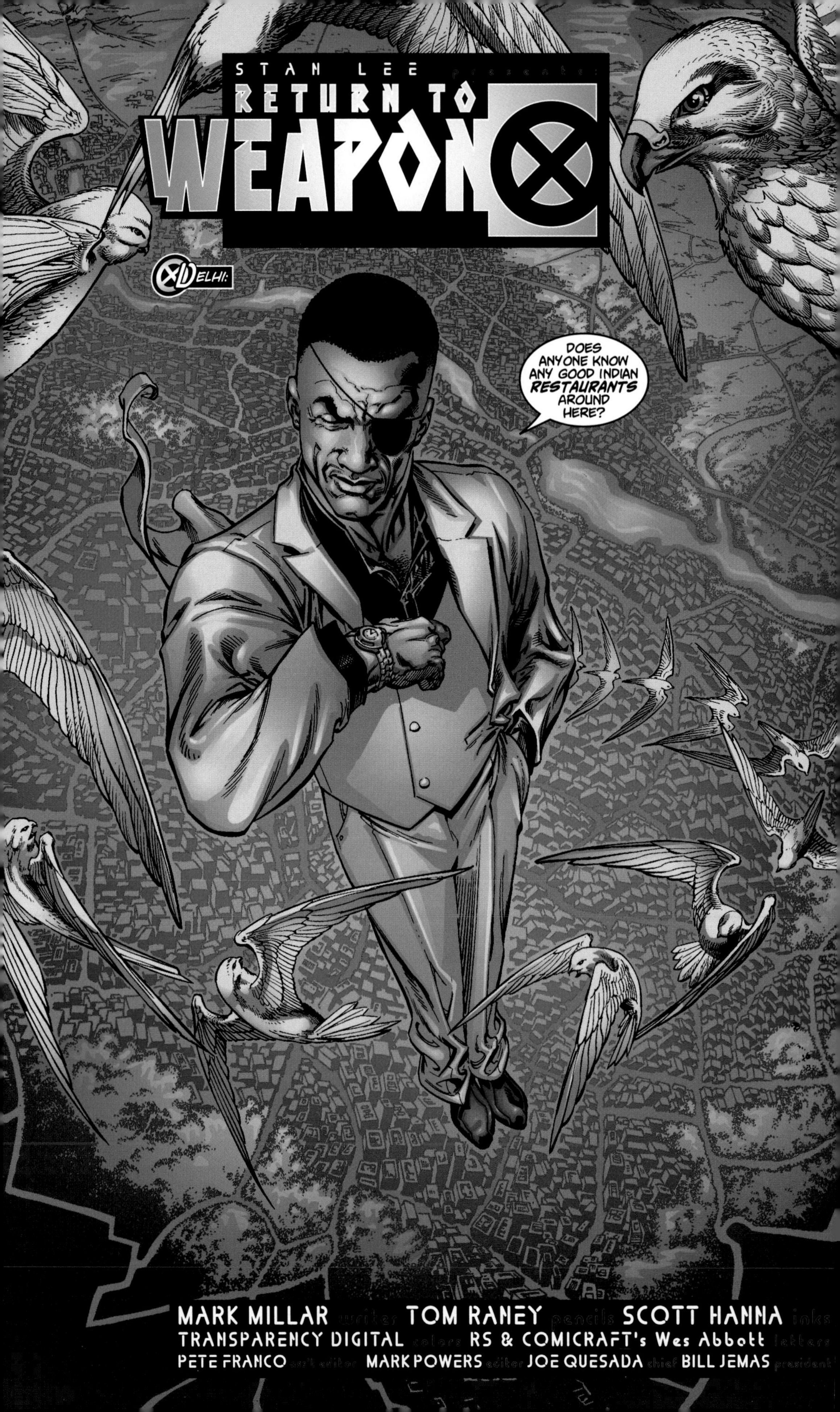
STAN LEE presents:
RETURN TO WEAPON X
DELHI:
DOES ANYONE KNOW ANY GOOD INDIAN RESTAURANTS AROUND HERE?
MARK MILLAR writer TOM RANEY pencils SCOTT HANNA inks
TRANSPARENCY DIGITAL colors RS & COMICRAFT's Wes Abbott letters
PETE FRANCO ass't editor MARK POWERS editor JOE QUESADA chief BILL JEMAS president

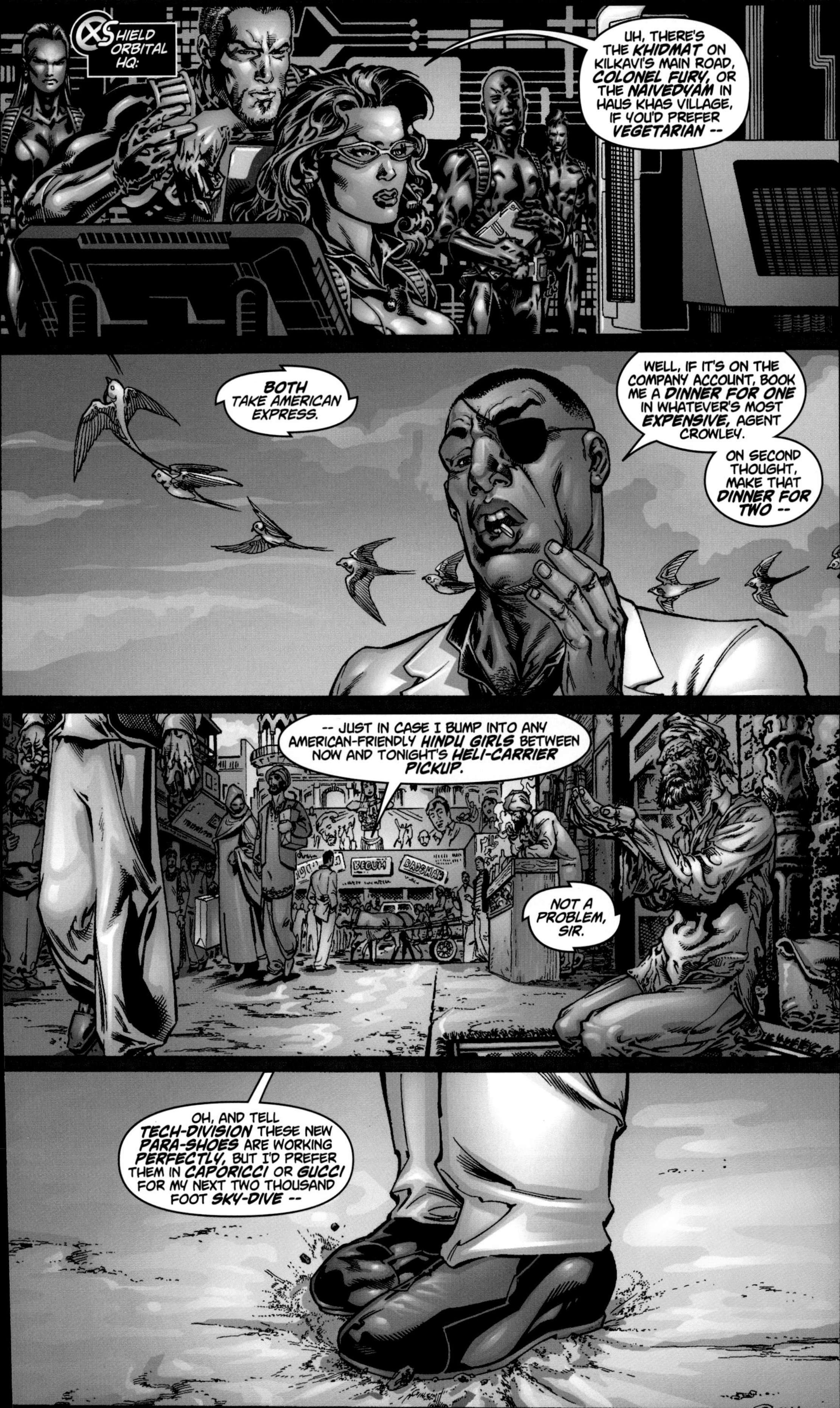

SHIELD ORBITAL HQ:
UH, THERE'S THE KHIDMAT ON KILKAVI'S MAIN ROAD, COLONEL FURY, OR THE NAIVEDYAM IN HAUS KHAS VILLAGE, IF YOU'D PREFER VEGETARIAN --
BOTH TAKE AMERICAN EXPRESS.
WELL, IF IT'S ON THE COMPANY ACCOUNT, BOOK ME A DINNER FOR ONE IN WHATEVER'S MOST EXPENSIVE, AGENT CROWLEY.
ON SECOND THOUGHT, MAKE THAT DINNER FOR TWO --
-- JUST IN CASE I BUMP INTO ANY AMERICAN-FRIENDLY HINDU GIRLS BETWEEN NOW AND TONIGHT'S HELI-CARRIER PICKUP.
BEGUM
BADSHAH
NOT A PROBLEM, SIR.
OH, AND TELL TECH-DIVISION THESE NEW PARA-SHOES ARE WORKING PERFECTLY, BUT I'D PREFER THEM IN CAPORICCI OR GUCCI FOR MY NEXT TWO THOUSAND FOOT SKY-DIVE --

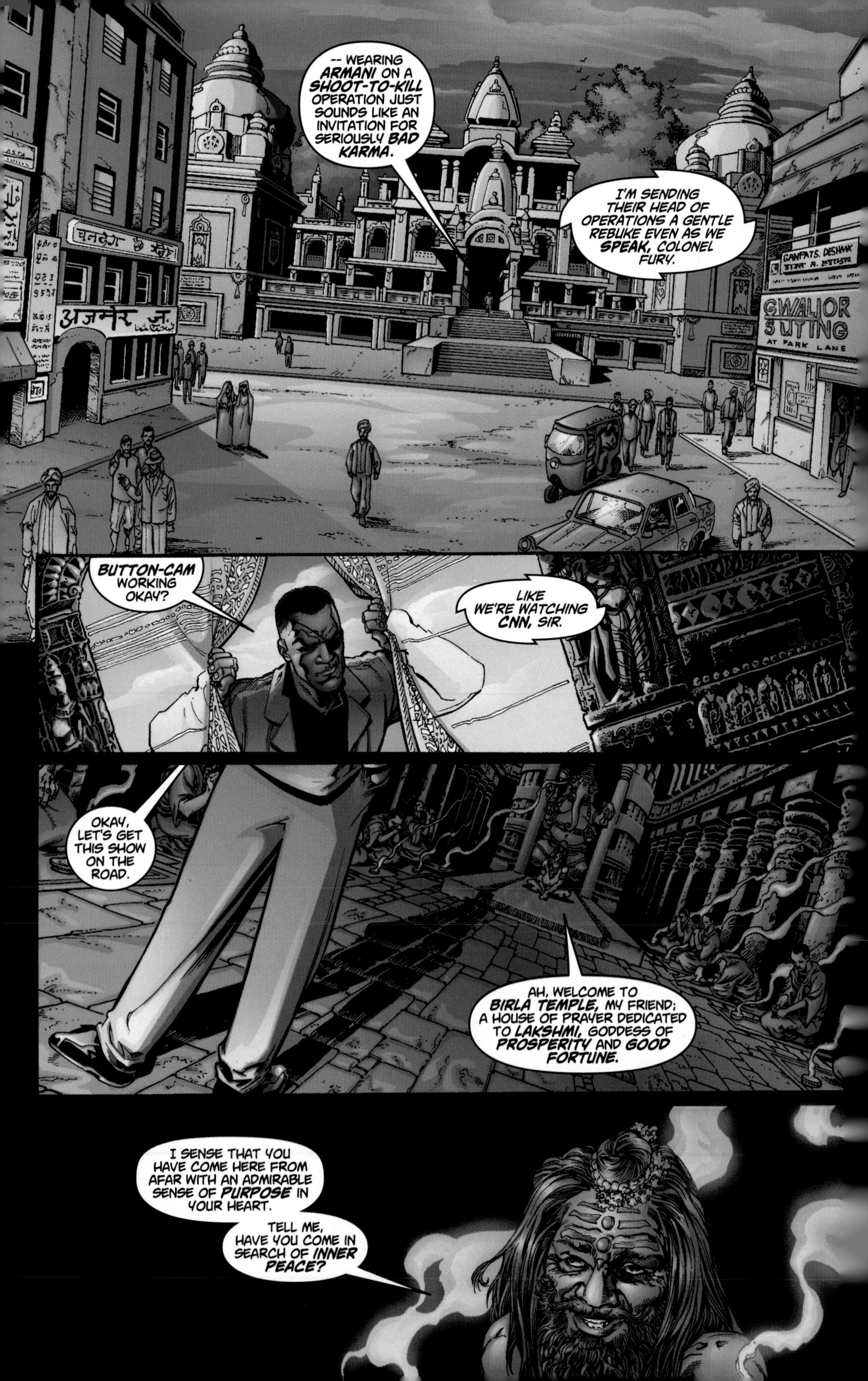
-- WEARING ARMANI ON A SHOOT-TO-KILL OPERATION JUST SOUNDS LIKE AN INVITATION FOR SERIOUSLY BAD KARMA.
I'M SENDING THEIR HEAD OF OPERATIONS A GENTLE REBUKE EVEN AS WE SPEAK, COLONEL FURY.
GANPATS. DESHAK
GWALIOR SUTING
AT PARK LANE
BUTTON-CAM WORKING OKAY?
LIKE WE'RE WATCHING CNN, SIR.
OKAY, LET'S GET THIS SHOW ON THE ROAD.
AH, WELCOME TO BIRLA TEMPLE, MY FRIEND; A HOUSE OF PRAYER DEDICATED TO LAKSHMI, GODDESS OF PROSPERITY AND GOOD FORTUNE.
I SENSE THAT YOU HAVE COME HERE FROM AFAR WITH AN ADMIRABLE SENSE OF PURPOSE IN YOUR HEART.
TELL ME, HAVE YOU COME IN SEARCH OF INNER PEACE?

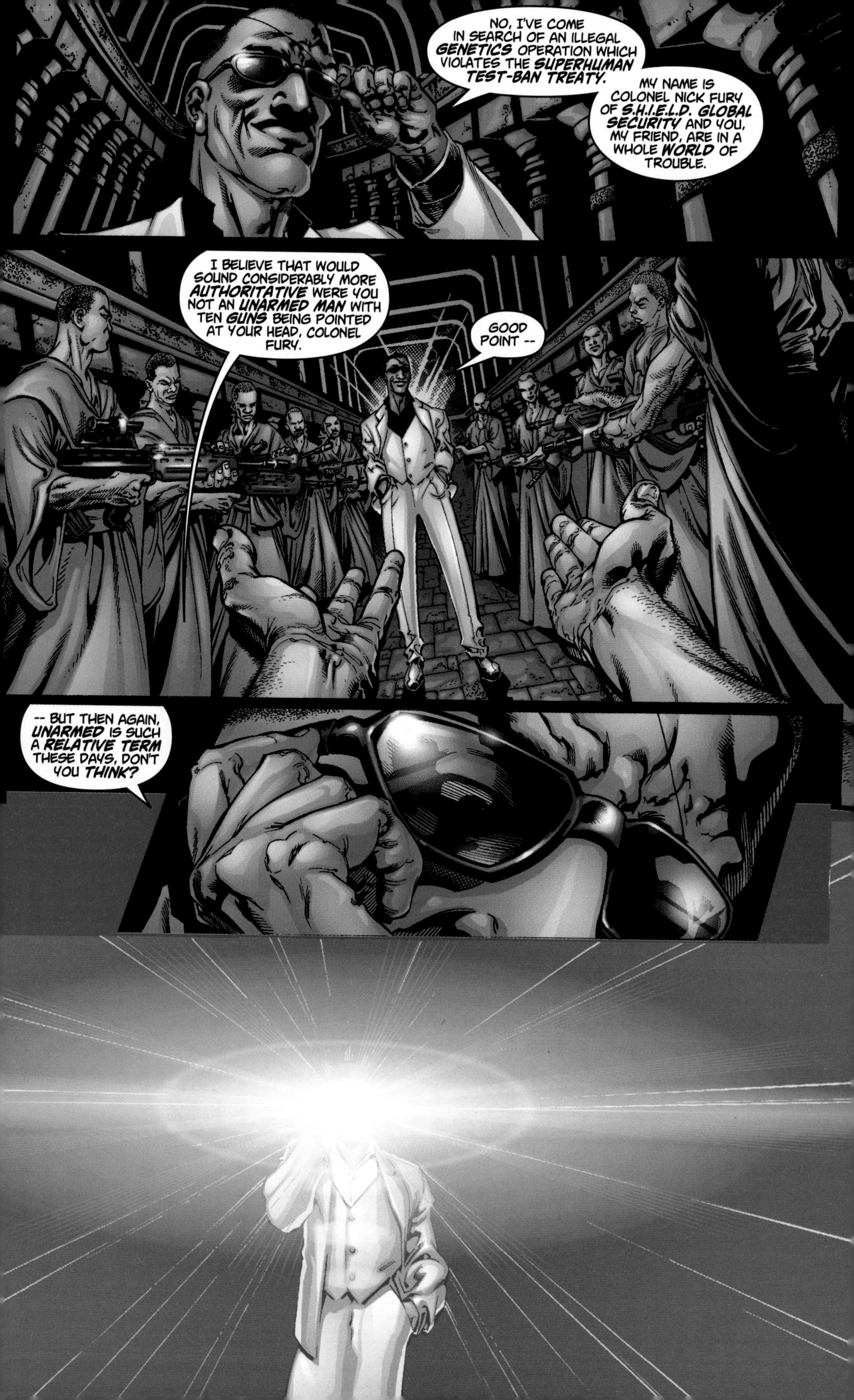
NO, I'VE COME IN SEARCH OF AN ILLEGAL GENETICS OPERATION WHICH VIOLATES THE SUPERHUMAN TEST-BAN TREATY.
MY NAME IS COLONEL NICK FURY OF S.H.I.E.L.D. GLOBAL SECURITY AND YOU, MY FRIEND, ARE IN A WHOLE WORLD OF TROUBLE.
I BELIEVE THAT WOULD SOUND CONSIDERABLY MORE AUTHORITATIVE WERE YOU NOT AN UNARMED MAN WITH TEN GUNS BEING POINTED AT YOUR HEAD, COLONEL FURY.
GOOD POINT --
-- BUT THEN AGAIN, UNARMED IS SUCH A RELATIVE TERM THESE DAYS, DON'T YOU THINK?

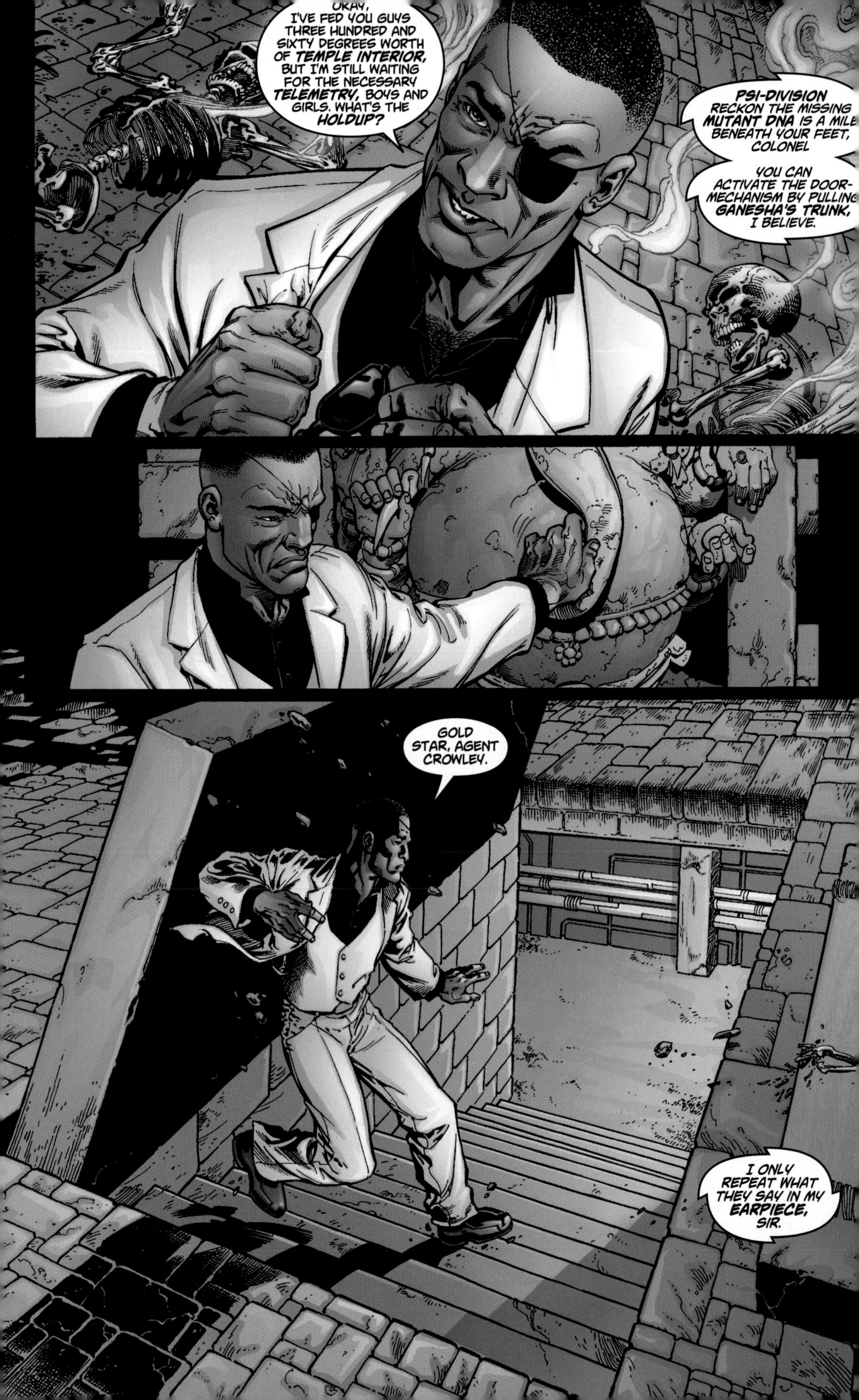
OKAY, I'VE FED YOU GUYS THREE HUNDRED AND SIXTY DEGREES WORTH OF TEMPLE INTERIOR, BUT I'M STILL WAITING FOR THE NECESSARY TELEMETRY, BOYS AND GIRLS. WHAT'S THE HOLDUP?
PSI-DIVISION RECKON THE MISSING MUTANT DNA IS A MILE BENEATH YOUR FEET, COLONEL
YOU CAN ACTIVATE THE DOOR-MECHANISM BY PULLING GANESHA'S TRUNK, I BELIEVE.
GOLD STAR, AGENT CROWLEY.
I ONLY REPEAT WHAT THEY SAY IN MY EARPIECE, SIR.

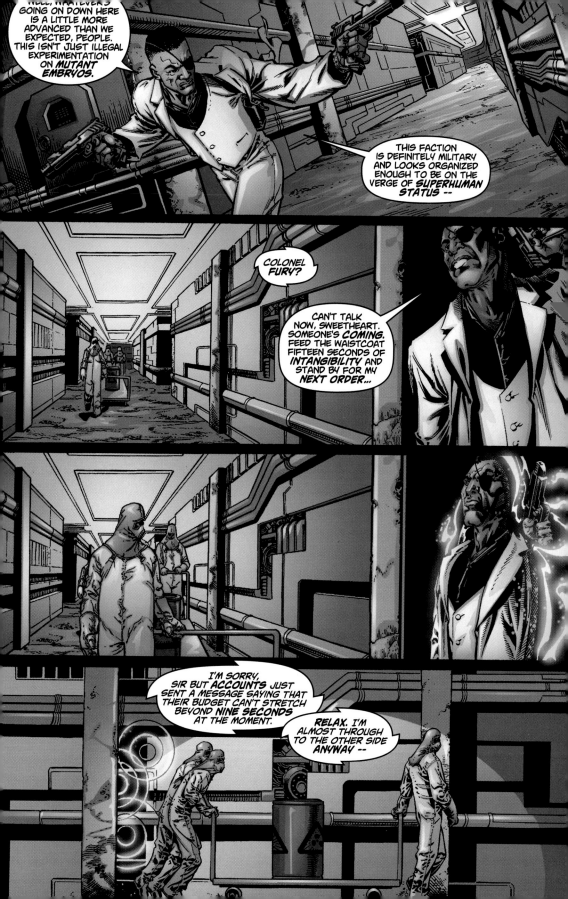

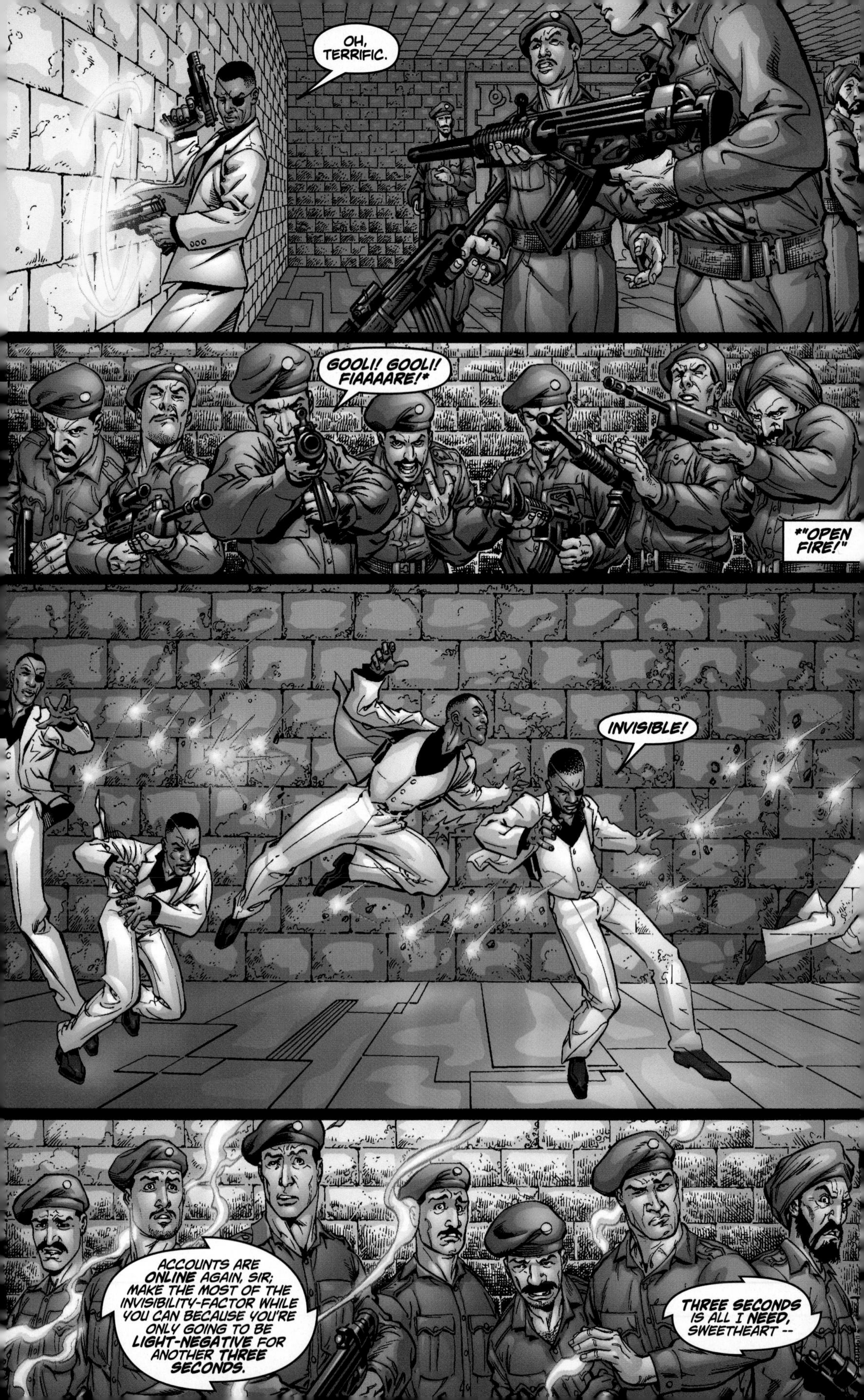
OH, TERRIFIC.
GOOLI! GOOLI! FIAAAARE!*
*"OPEN FIRE!"
INVISIBLE!
ACCOUNTS ARE ONLINE AGAIN, SIR; MAKE THE MOST OF THE INVISIBILITY-FACTOR WHILE YOU CAN BECAUSE YOU'RE ONLY GOING TO BE LIGHT-NEGATIVE FOR ANOTHER THREE SECONDS.
THREE SECONDS IS ALL I NEED, SWEETHEART --

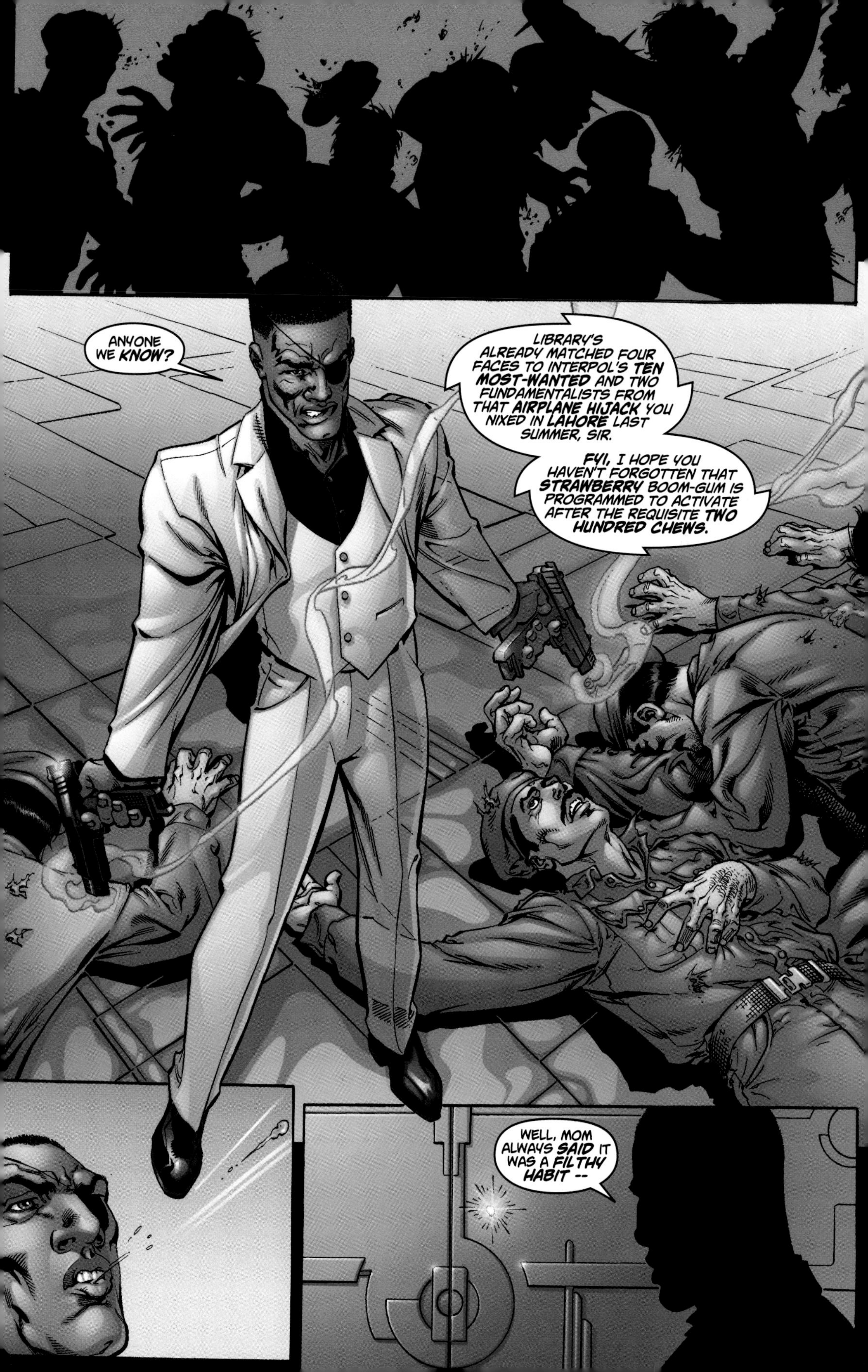
ANYONE WE KNOW?
LIBRARY'S ALREADY MATCHED FOUR FACES TO INTERPOL'S TEN MOST-WANTED AND TWO FUNDAMENTALISTS FROM THAT AIRPLANE HIJACK YOU NIXED IN LAHORE LAST SUMMER, SIR.
FYI, I HOPE YOU HAVEN'T FORGOTTEN THAT STRAWBERRY BOOM-GUM IS PROGRAMMED TO ACTIVATE AFTER THE REQUISITE TWO HUNDRED CHEWS.
WELL, MOM ALWAYS SAID IT WAS A FILTHY HABIT --

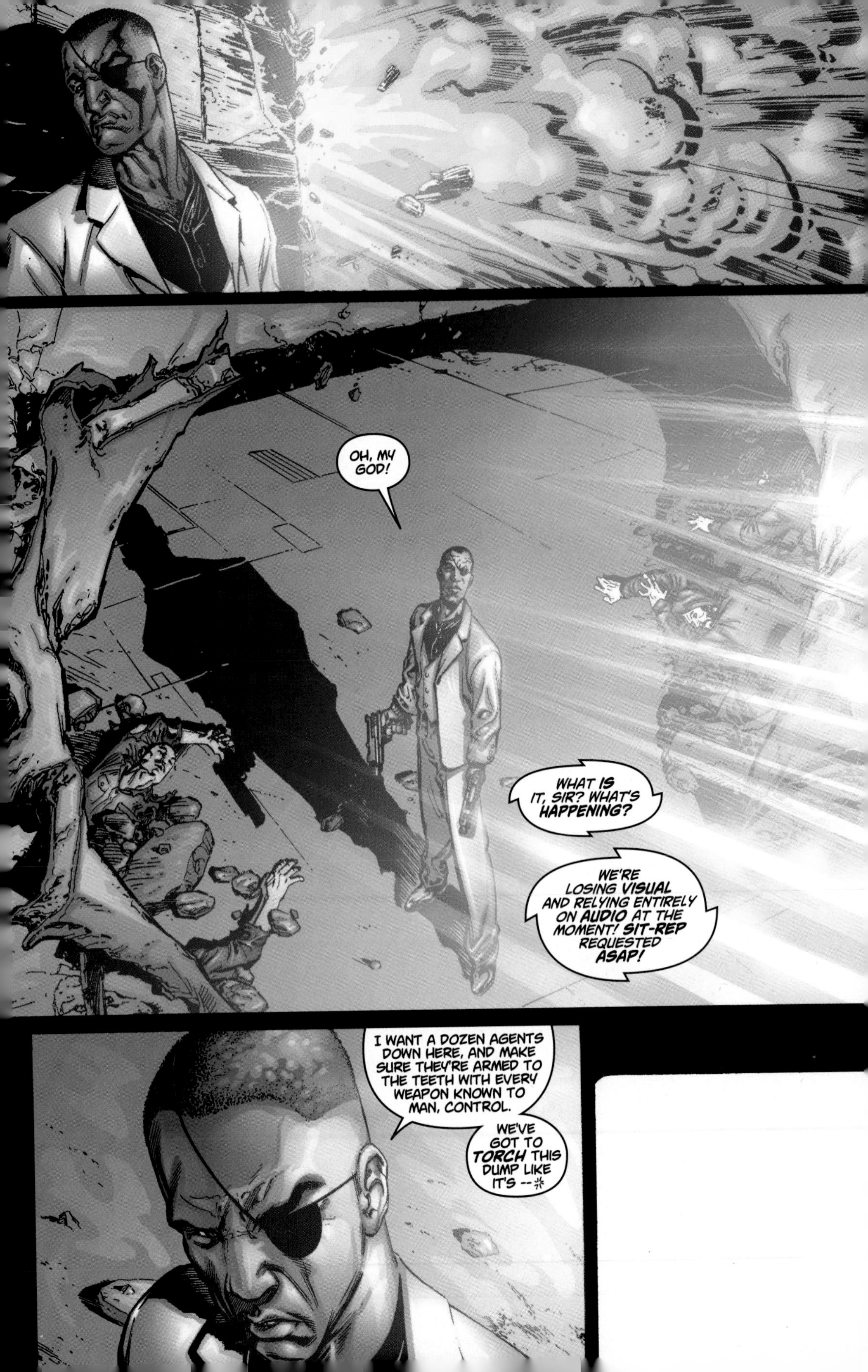
OH, MY GOD!
WHAT IS IT, SIR? WHAT'S HAPPENING?
WE'RE LOSING VISUAL AND RELYING ENTIRELY ON AUDIO AT THE MOMENT! SIT-REP REQUESTED ASAP!
I WANT A DOZEN AGENTS DOWN HERE, AND MAKE SURE THEY'RE ARMED TO THE TEETH WITH EVERY WEAPON KNOWN TO MAN, CONTROL.
WE'VE GOT TO TORCH THIS DUMP LIKE IT'S --

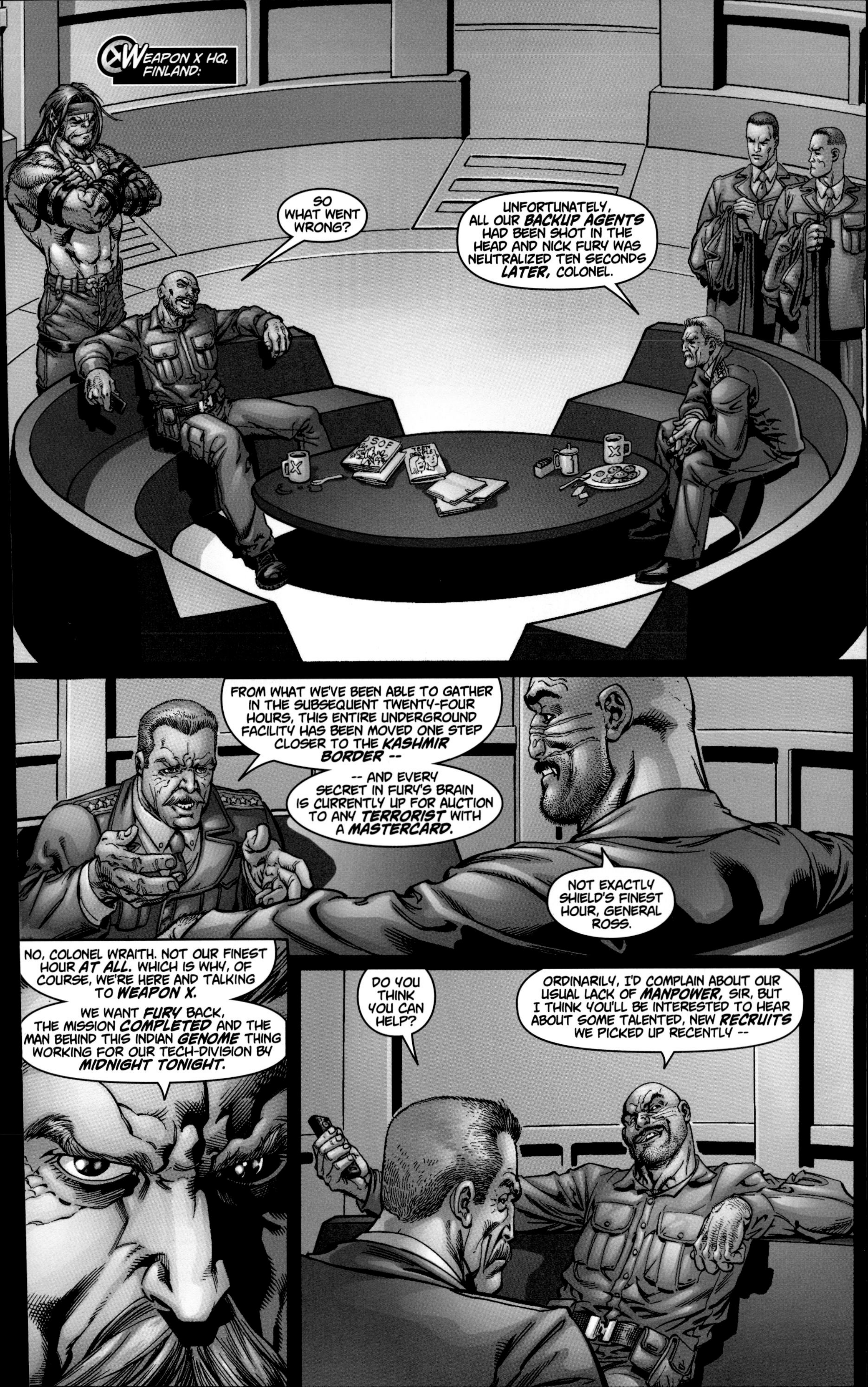
WEAPON X HQ, FINLAND:
SO WHAT WENT WRONG?
UNFORTUNATELY, ALL OUR BACKUP AGENTS HAD BEEN SHOT IN THE HEAD AND NICK FURY WAS NEUTRALIZED TEN SECONDS LATER, COLONEL.
FROM WHAT WE'VE BEEN ABLE TO GATHER IN THE SUBSEQUENT TWENTY-FOUR HOURS, THIS ENTIRE UNDERGROUND FACILITY HAS BEEN MOVED ONE STEP CLOSER TO THE KASHMIR BORDER --
-- AND EVERY SECRET IN FURY'S BRAIN IS CURRENTLY UP FOR AUCTION TO ANY TERRORIST WITH A MASTERCARD.
NOT EXACTLY SHIELD'S FINEST HOUR, GENERAL ROSS.
NO, COLONEL WRAITH. NOT OUR FINEST HOUR AT ALL. WHICH IS WHY, OF COURSE, WE'RE HERE AND TALKING TO WEAPON X.
WE WANT FURY BACK, THE MISSION COMPLETED AND THE MAN BEHIND THIS INDIAN GENOME THING WORKING FOR OUR TECH-DIVISION BY MIDNIGHT TONIGHT.
DO YOU THINK YOU CAN HELP?
ORDINARILY, I'D COMPLAIN ABOUT OUR USUAL LACK OF MANPOWER, SIR, BUT I THINK YOU'LL BE INTERESTED TO HEAR ABOUT SOME TALENTED, NEW RECRUITS WE PICKED UP RECENTLY --

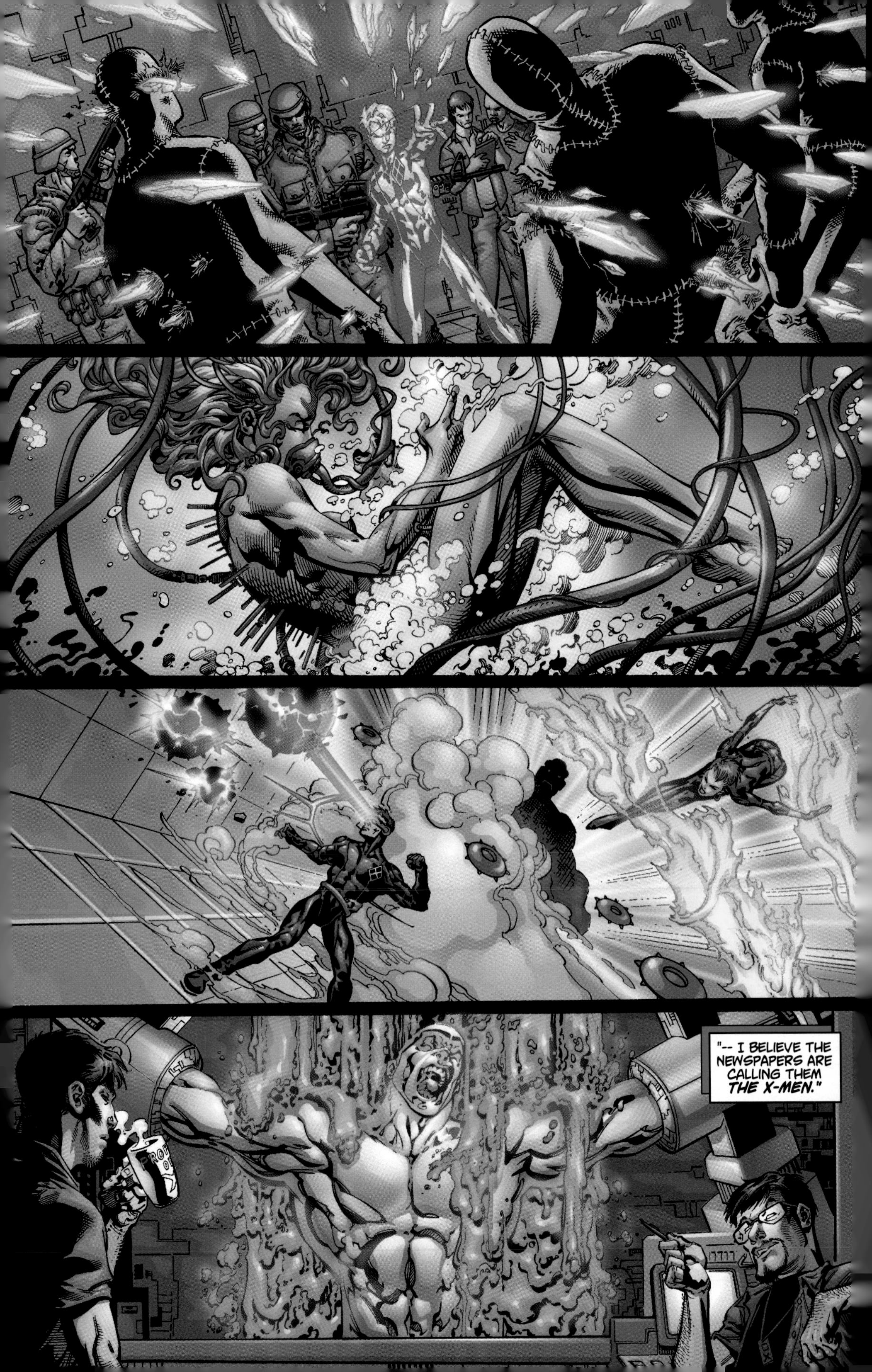
"-- I BELIEVE THE NEWSPAPERS ARE CALLING THEM *THE X-MEN.*"

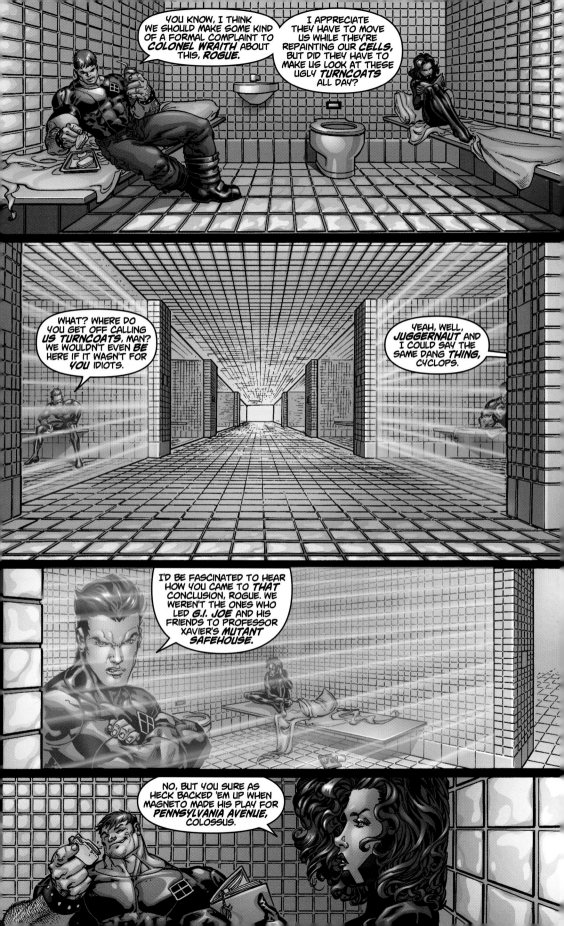

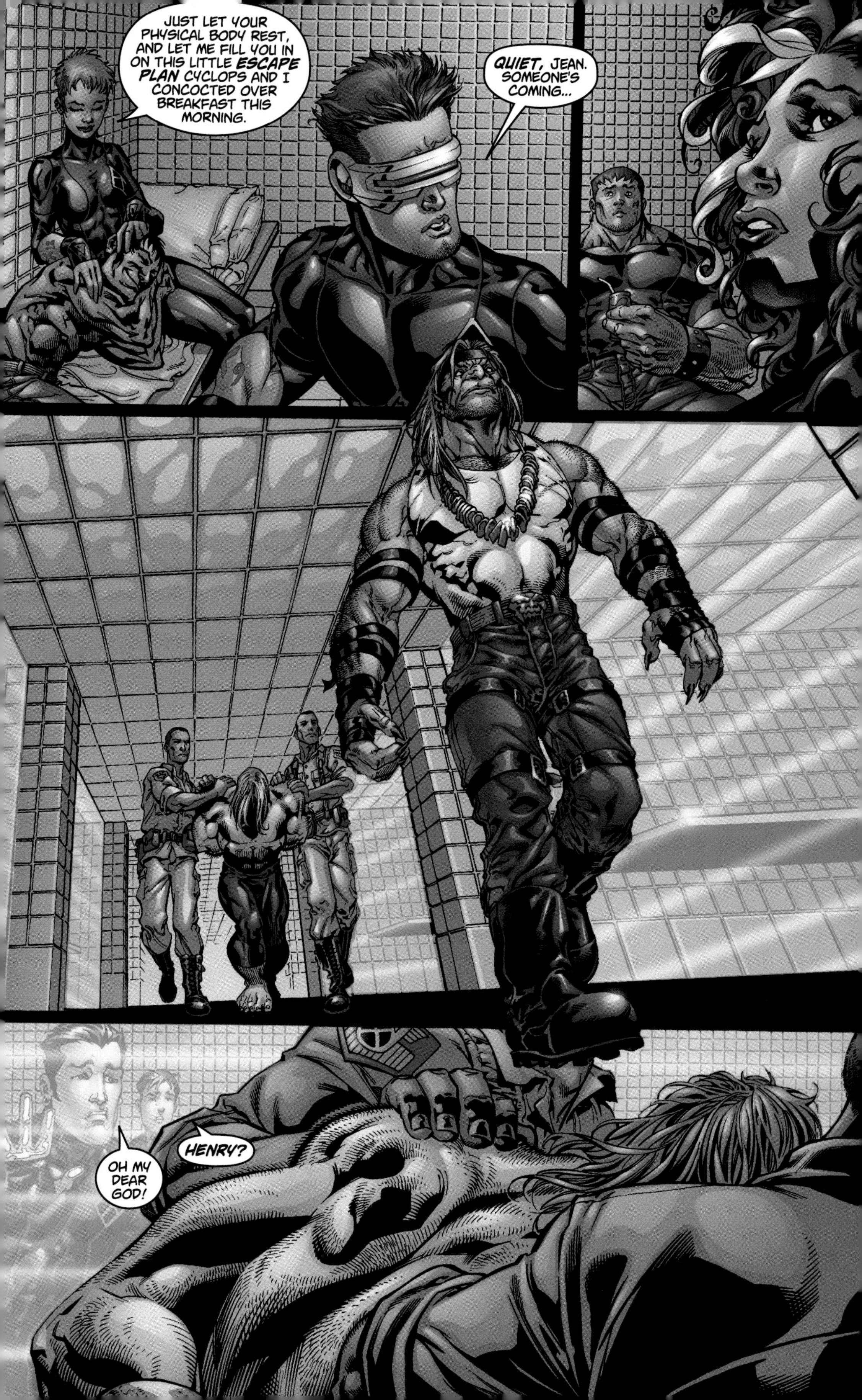
JUST LET YOUR PHYSICAL BODY REST, AND LET ME FILL YOU IN ON THIS LITTLE ESCAPE PLAN CYCLOPS AND I CONCOCTED OVER BREAKFAST THIS MORNING.
QUIET, JEAN. SOMEONE'S COMING...
HENRY?
OH MY DEAR GOD!

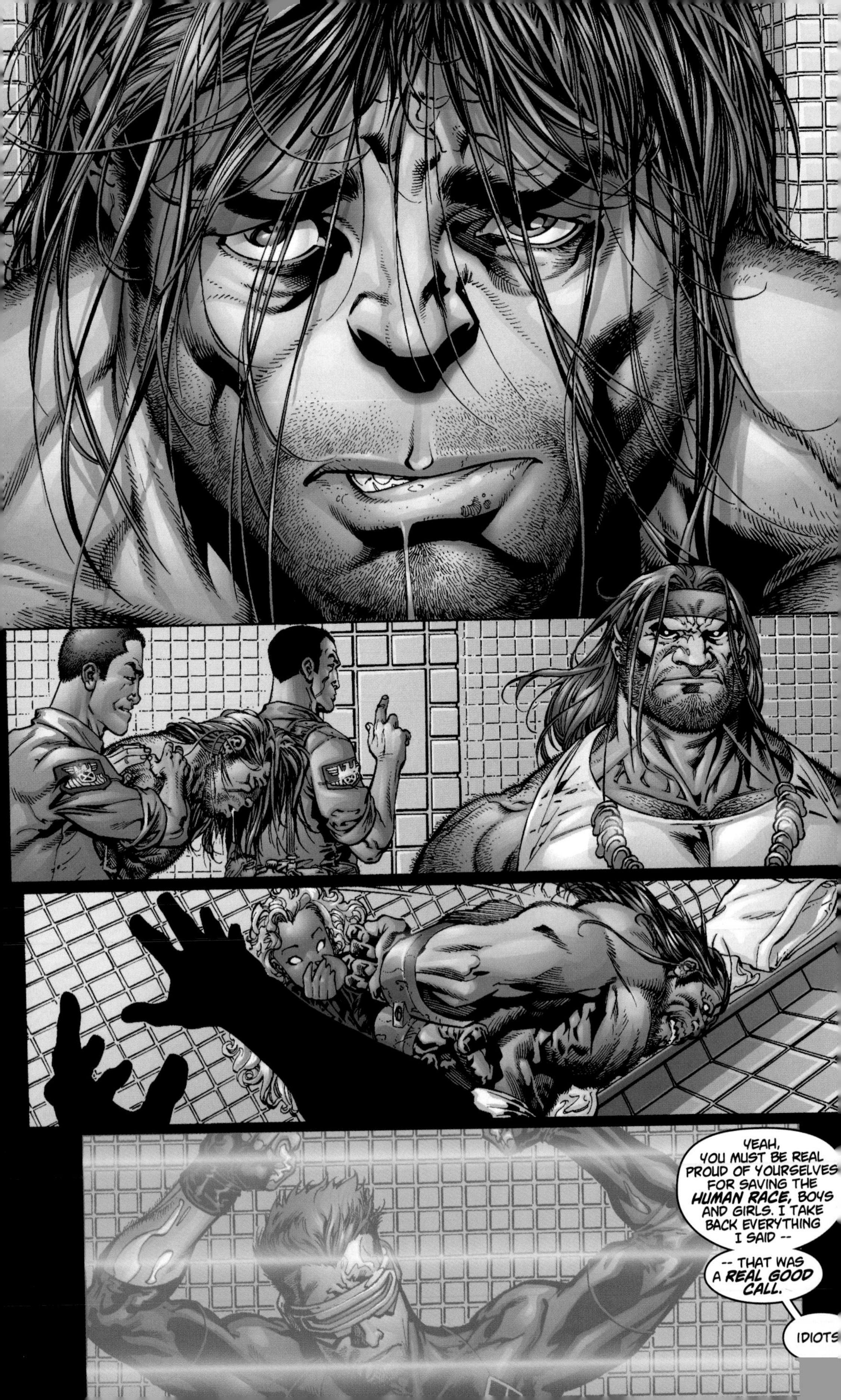
YEAH, YOU MUST BE REAL PROUD OF YOURSELVES FOR SAVING THE HUMAN RACE, BOYS AND GIRLS. I TAKE BACK EVERYTHING I SAID --
-- THAT WAS A REAL GOOD CALL.
IDIOTS

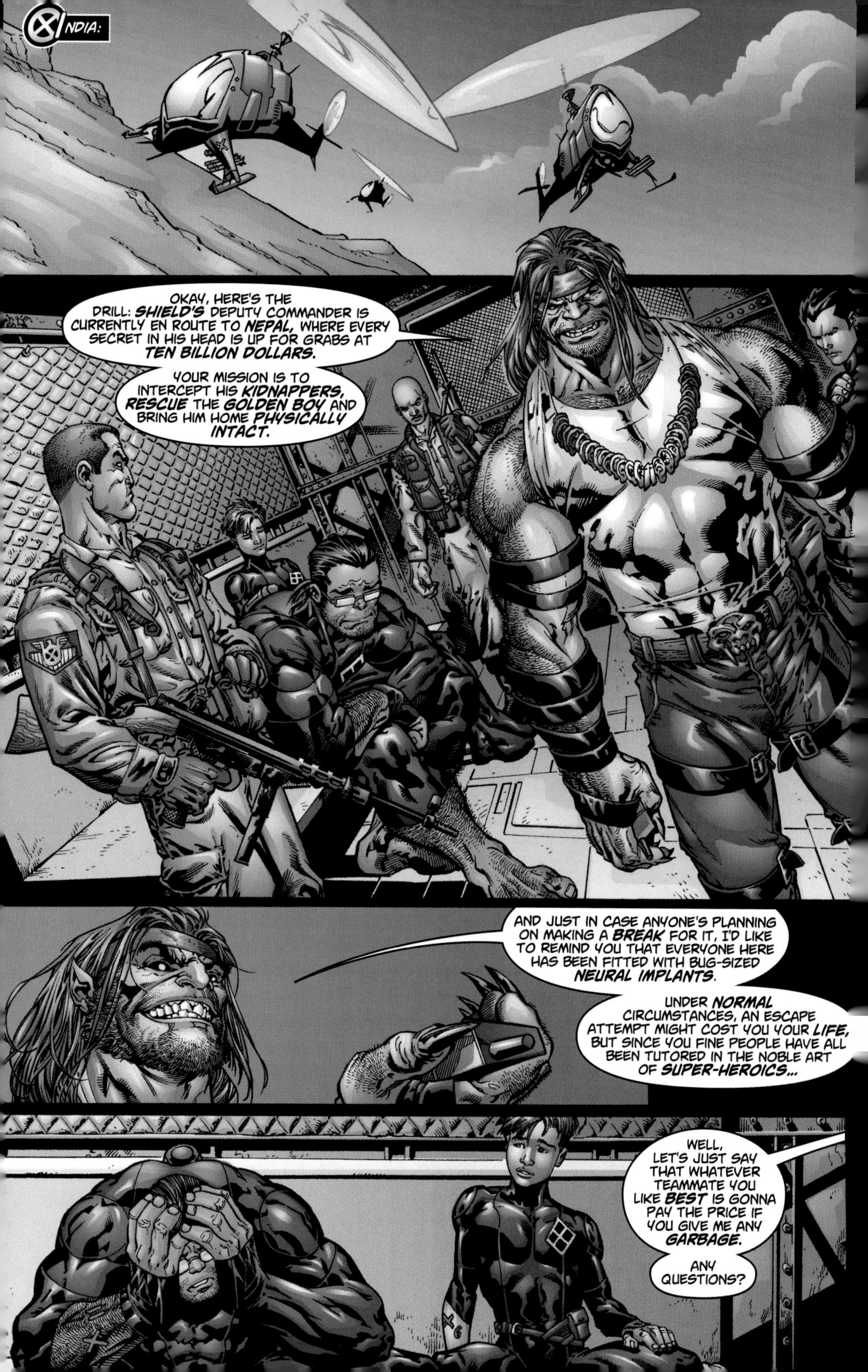
INDIA:
OKAY, HERE'S THE DRILL: SHIELD'S DEPUTY COMMANDER IS CURRENTLY EN ROUTE TO NEPAL, WHERE EVERY SECRET IN HIS HEAD IS UP FOR GRABS AT TEN BILLION DOLLARS.
YOUR MISSION IS TO INTERCEPT HIS KIDNAPPERS, RESCUE THE GOLDEN BOY AND BRING HIM HOME PHYSICALLY INTACT.
AND JUST IN CASE ANYONE'S PLANNING ON MAKING A BREAK FOR IT, I'D LIKE TO REMIND YOU THAT EVERYONE HERE HAS BEEN FITTED WITH BUG-SIZED NEURAL IMPLANTS.
UNDER NORMAL CIRCUMSTANCES, AN ESCAPE ATTEMPT MIGHT COST YOU YOUR LIFE, BUT SINCE YOU FINE PEOPLE HAVE ALL BEEN TUTORED IN THE NOBLE ART OF SUPER-HEROICS...
WELL, LET'S JUST SAY THAT WHATEVER TEAMMATE YOU LIKE BEST IS GONNA PAY THE PRICE IF YOU GIVE ME ANY GARBAGE.
ANY QUESTIONS?

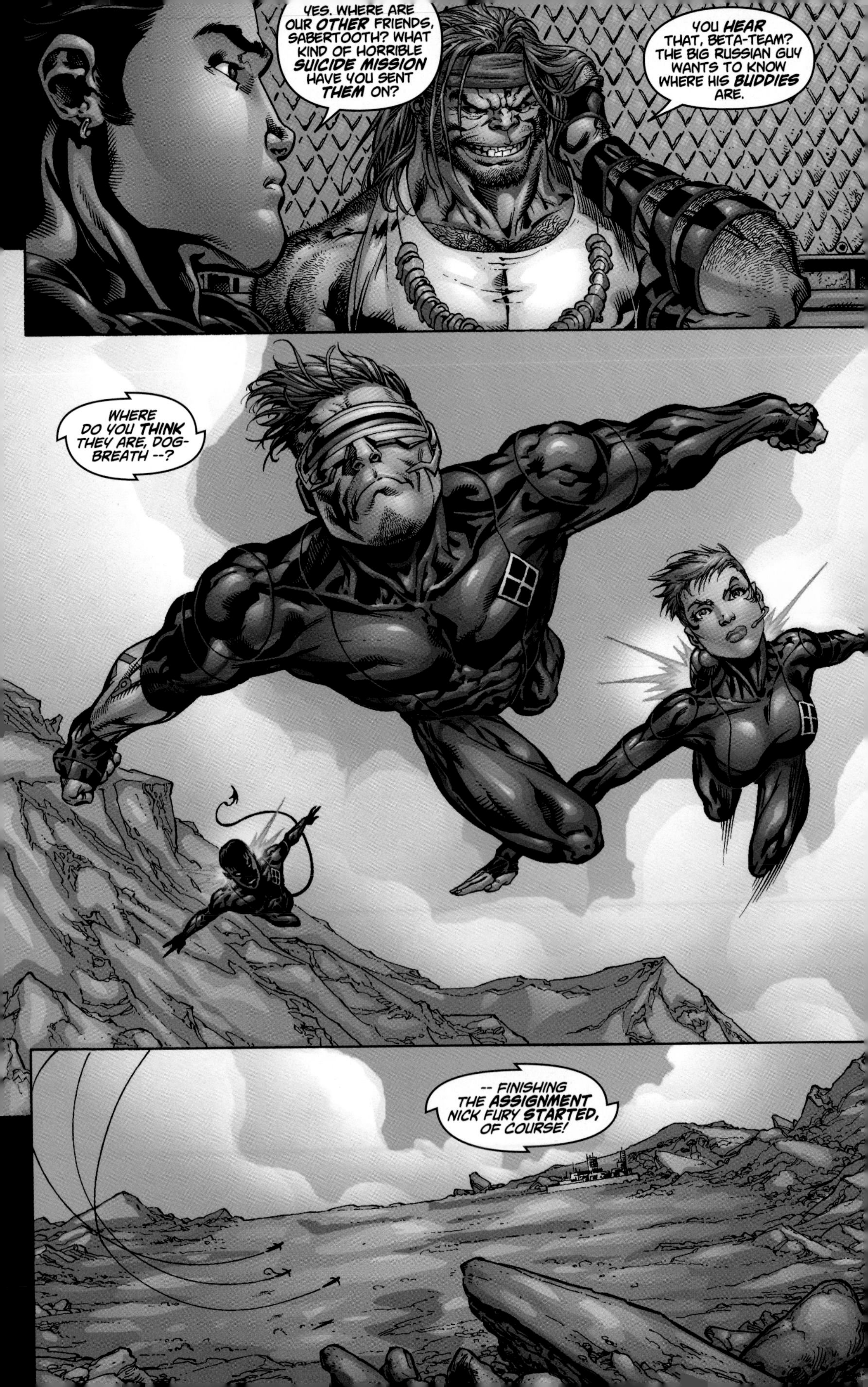

YES. WHERE ARE OUR OTHER FRIENDS, SABERTOOTH? WHAT KIND OF HORRIBLE SUICIDE MISSION HAVE YOU SENT THEM ON?
YOU HEAR THAT, BETA-TEAM? THE BIG RUSSIAN GUY WANTS TO KNOW WHERE HIS BUDDIES ARE.
WHERE DO YOU THINK THEY ARE, DOG-BREATH --?
-- FINISHING THE ASSIGNMENT NICK FURY STARTED, OF COURSE!

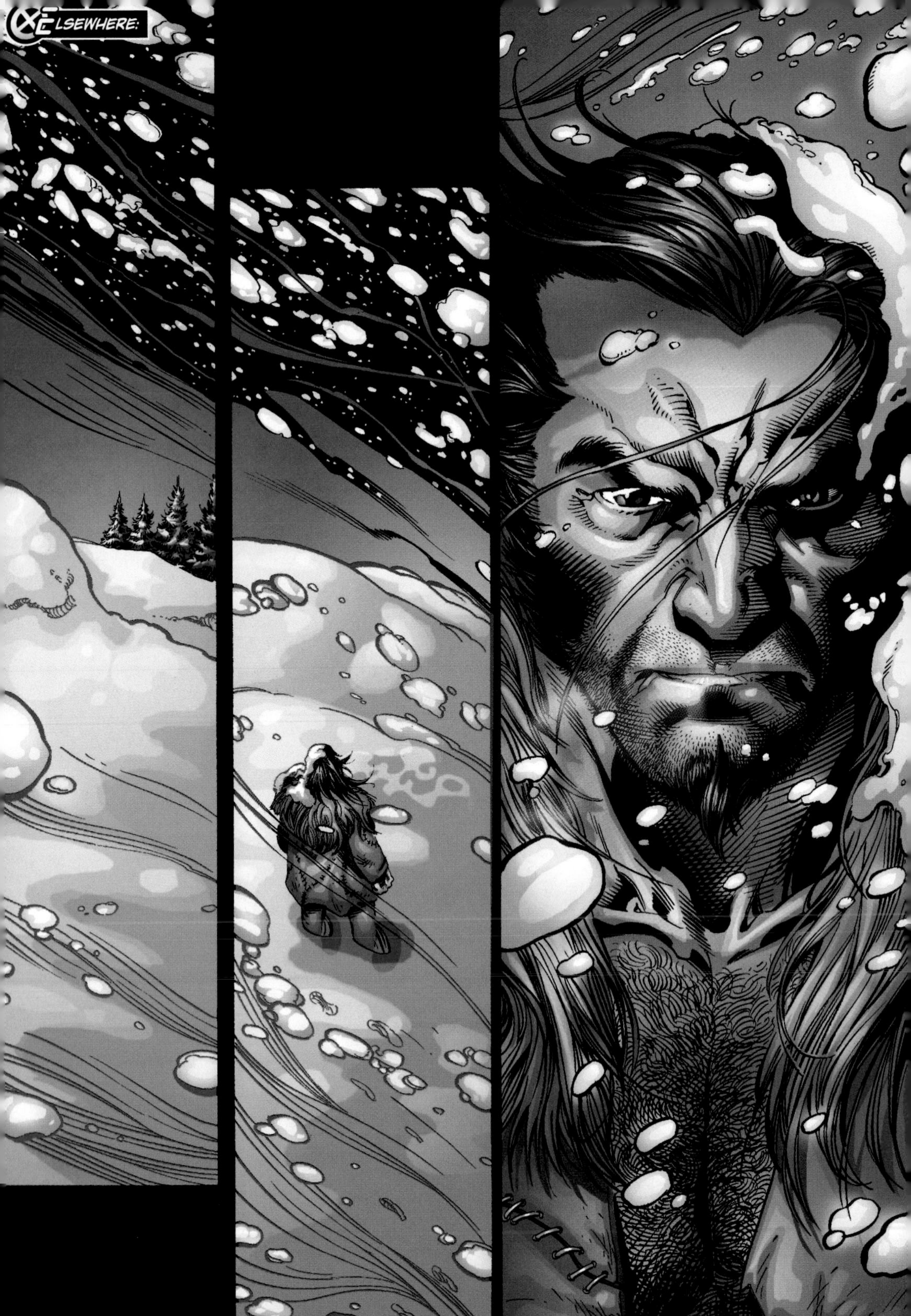
ELSEWHERE:

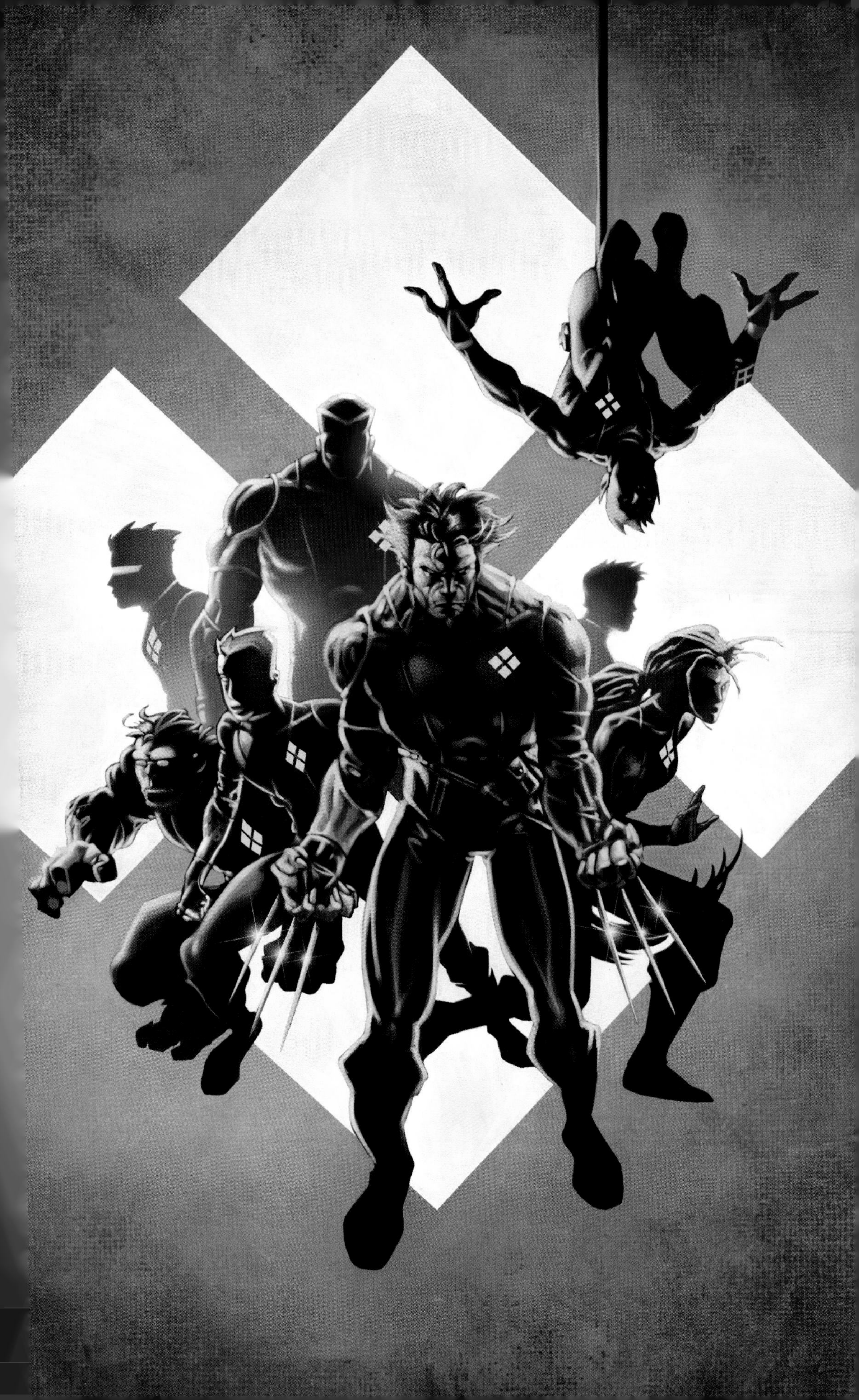

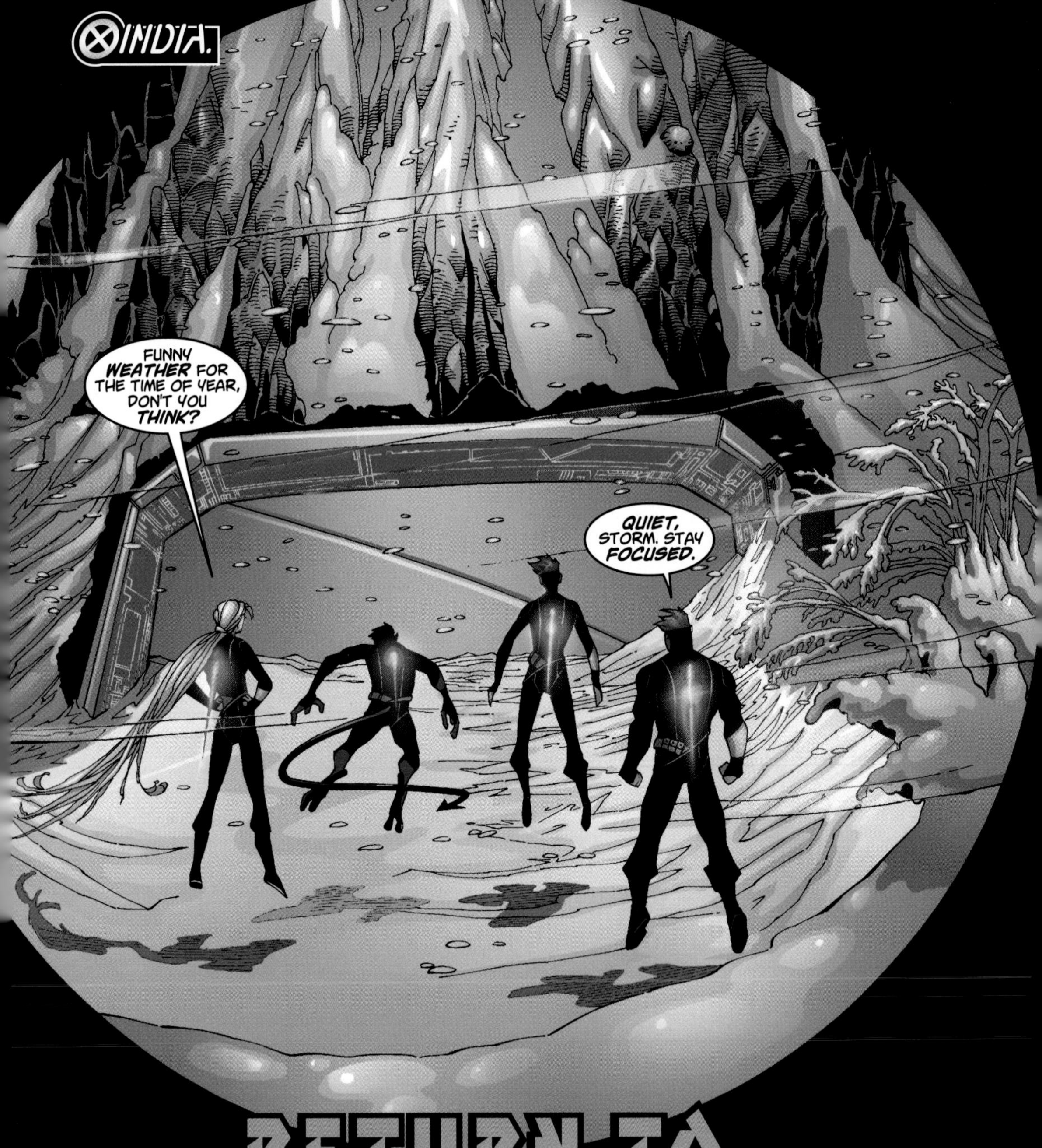
X INDIA.
FUNNY WEATHER FOR THE TIME OF YEAR, DON'T YOU THINK?
QUIET, STORM. STAY FOCUSED.

RETURN TO WEAPON X

PART FOUR OF SIX

MARK MILLAR writer ADAM KUBERT penciler ART THIBERT inker
TRANSPARENCY DIGITAL colors Richard Starkings & COMICRAFT's Saida! letters
PETE FRANCO ass't editor MARK POWERS editor JOE QUESADA chief BILL JEMAS president
a STAN LEE presentation!

?

IF IT'S ANY CONSOLATION, I REALLY AM INCREDIBLY *SORRY* ABOUT THIS, GENTLEMEN...

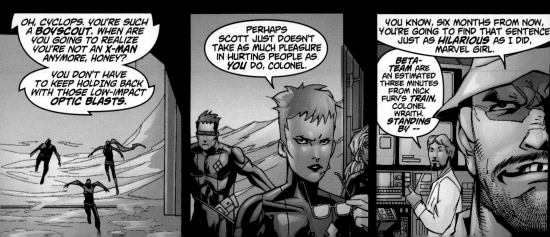

OH, CYCLOPS. YOU'RE SUCH A *BOYSCOUT.* WHEN ARE YOU GOING TO REALIZE YOU'RE NOT AN *X-MAN* ANYMORE, HONEY?

YOU DON'T HAVE TO KEEP HOLDING BACK WITH THOSE LOW-IMPACT *OPTIC BLASTS.*

PERHAPS SCOTT JUST DOESN'T TAKE AS MUCH PLEASURE IN HURTING PEOPLE AS *YOU* DO, COLONEL.

YOU KNOW, SIX MONTHS FROM NOW, YOU'RE GOING TO FIND THAT SENTENCE JUST AS *HILARIOUS* AS I DID, MARVEL GIRL.

BETA-TEAM ARE AN ESTIMATED THREE MINUTES FROM NICK FURY'S *TRAIN,* COLONEL WRAITH. *STANDING BY --*

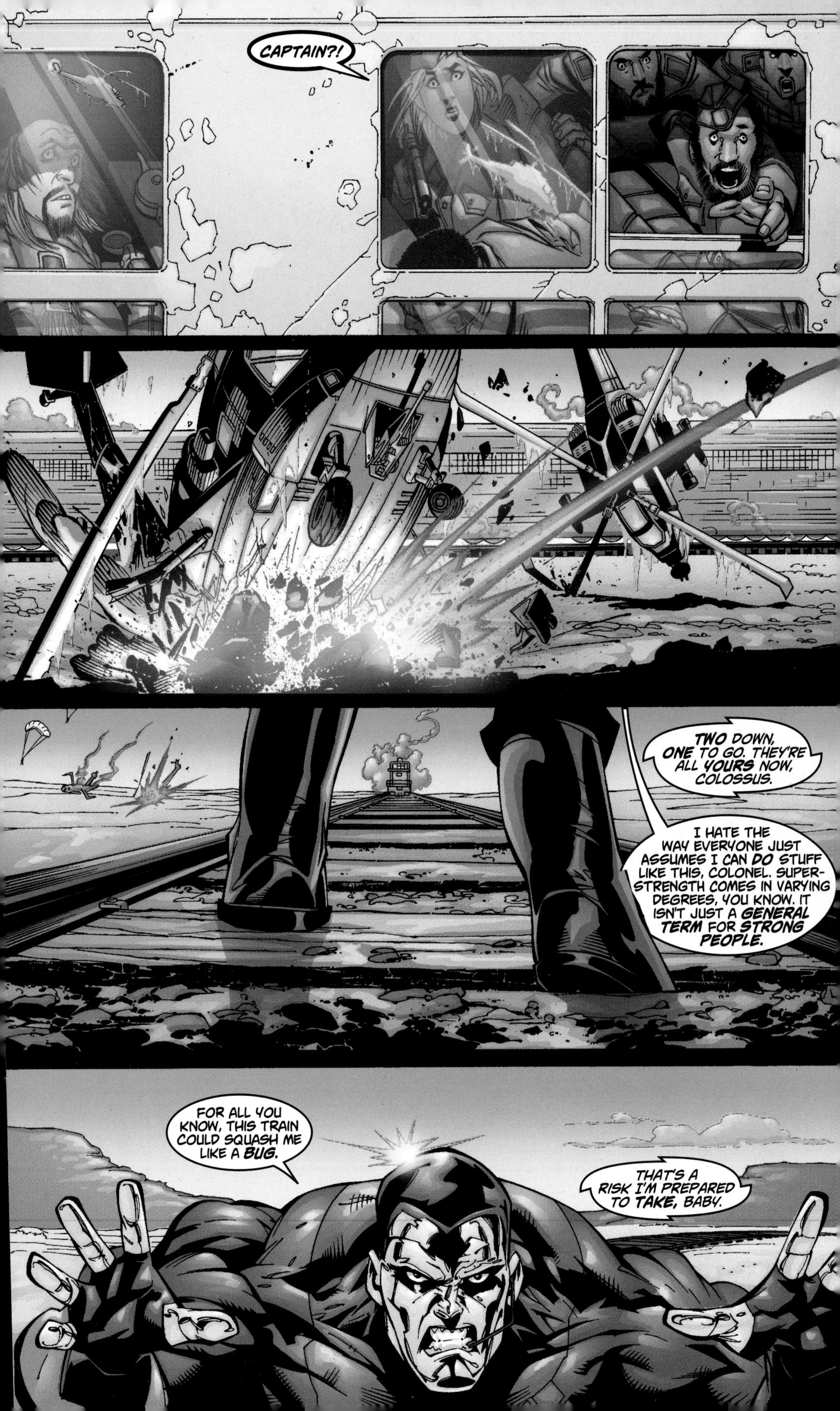
CAPTAIN?!
TWO DOWN, ONE TO GO. THEY'RE ALL YOURS NOW, COLOSSUS.
I HATE THE WAY EVERYONE JUST ASSUMES I CAN DO STUFF LIKE THIS, COLONEL. SUPER-STRENGTH COMES IN VARYING DEGREES, YOU KNOW. IT ISN'T JUST A GENERAL TERM FOR STRONG PEOPLE.
FOR ALL YOU KNOW, THIS TRAIN COULD SQUASH ME LIKE A BUG.
THAT'S A RISK I'M PREPARED TO TAKE, BABY.

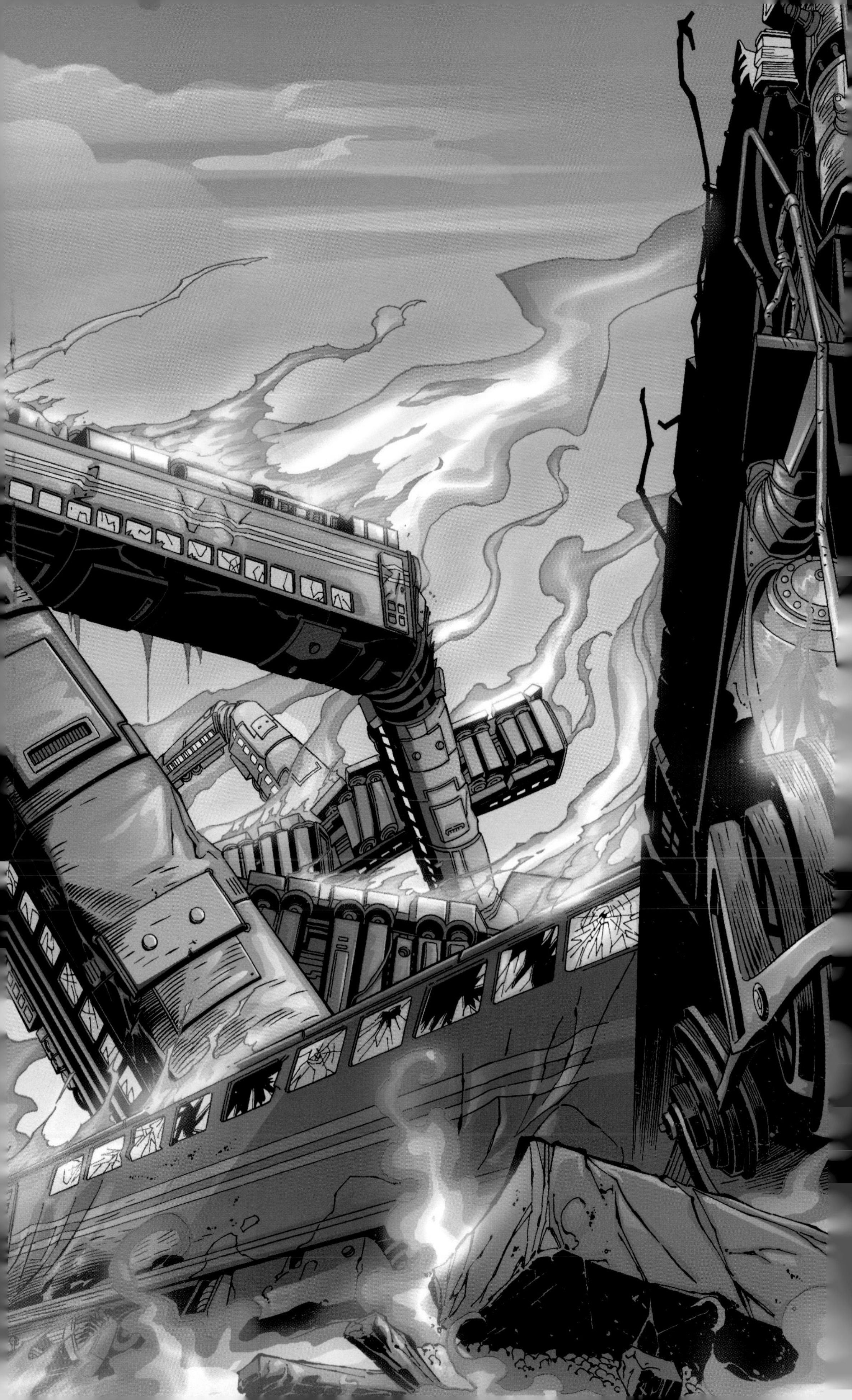

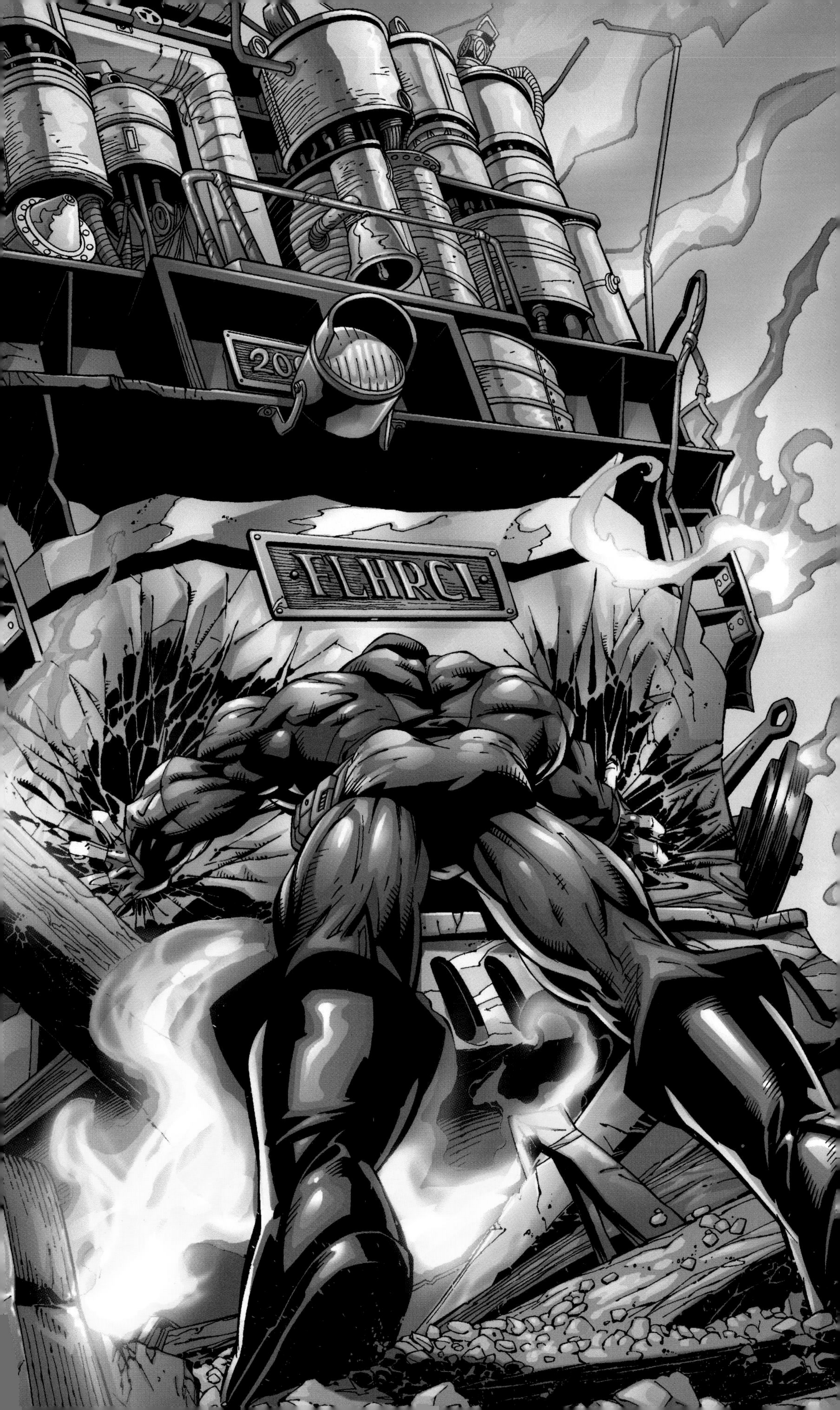
FLHRCI

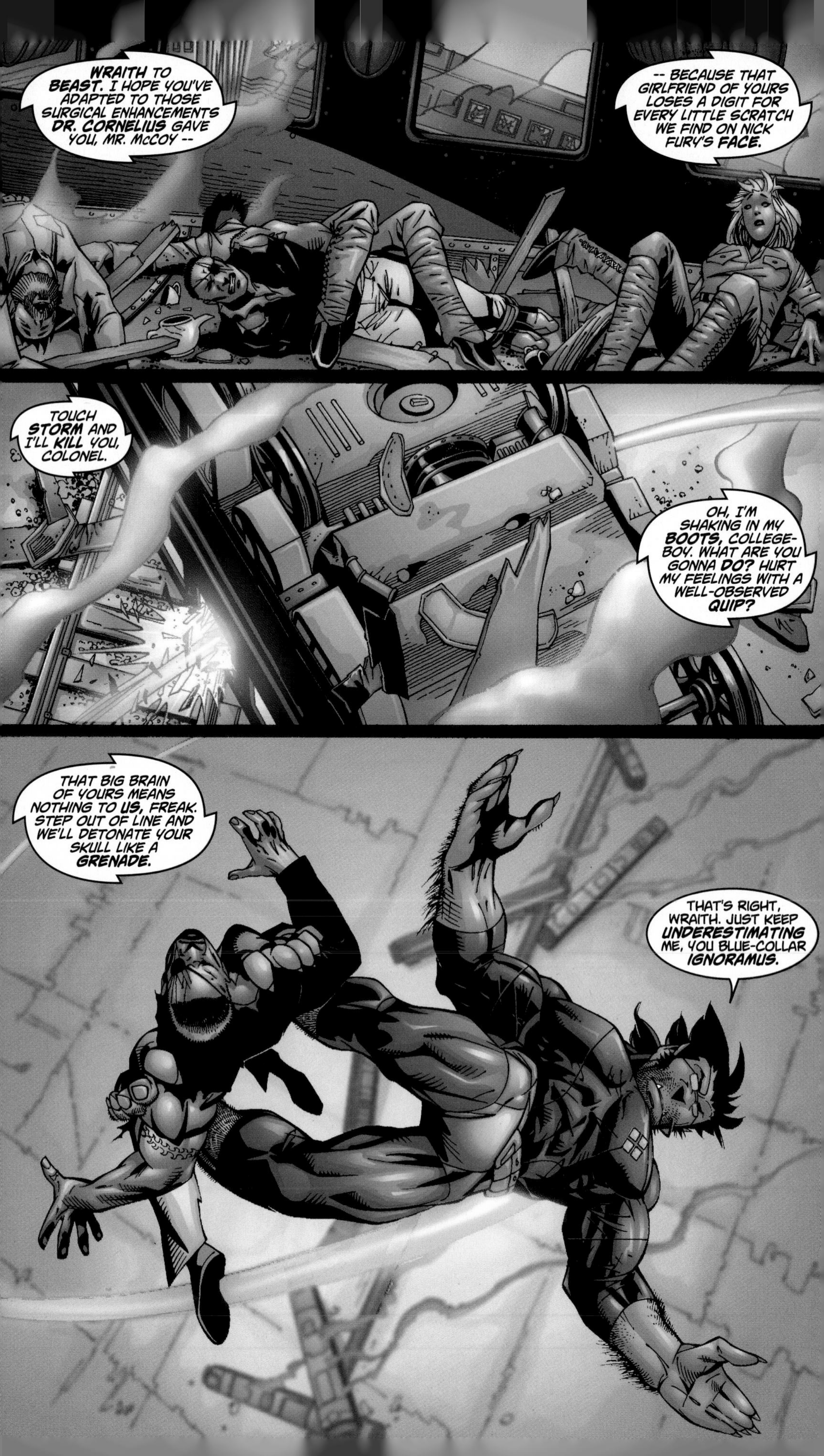
WRAITH TO BEAST. I HOPE YOU'VE ADAPTED TO THOSE SURGICAL ENHANCEMENTS DR. CORNELIUS GAVE YOU, MR. McCOY --
-- BECAUSE THAT GIRLFRIEND OF YOURS LOSES A DIGIT FOR EVERY LITTLE SCRATCH WE FIND ON NICK FURY'S FACE.
TOUCH STORM AND I'LL KILL YOU, COLONEL.
OH, I'M SHAKING IN MY BOOTS, COLLEGE-BOY. WHAT ARE YOU GONNA DO? HURT MY FEELINGS WITH A WELL-OBSERVED QUIP?
THAT BIG BRAIN OF YOURS MEANS NOTHING TO US, FREAK. STEP OUT OF LINE AND WE'LL DETONATE YOUR SKULL LIKE A GRENADE.
THAT'S RIGHT, WRAITH. JUST KEEP UNDERESTIMATING ME, YOU BLUE-COLLAR IGNORAMUS.

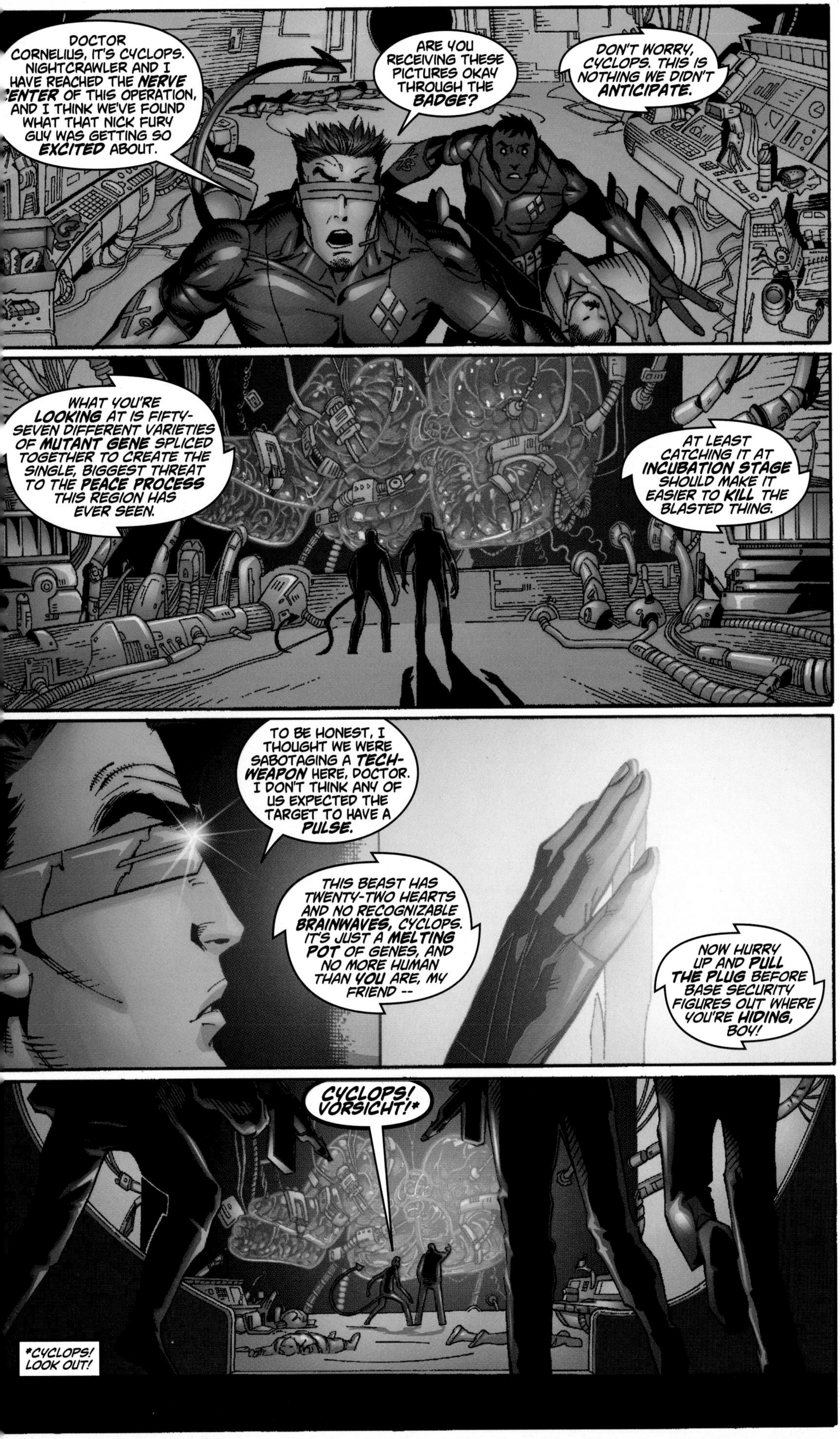
DOCTOR CORNELIUS, IT'S CYCLOPS. NIGHTCRAWLER AND I HAVE REACHED THE NERVE CENTER OF THIS OPERATION, AND I THINK WE'VE FOUND WHAT THAT NICK FURY GUY WAS GETTING SO EXCITED ABOUT.
ARE YOU RECEIVING THESE PICTURES OKAY THROUGH THE BADGE?
DON'T WORRY, CYCLOPS. THIS IS NOTHING WE DIDN'T ANTICIPATE.
WHAT YOU'RE LOOKING AT IS FIFTY-SEVEN DIFFERENT VARIETIES OF MUTANT GENE SPLICED TOGETHER TO CREATE THE SINGLE, BIGGEST THREAT TO THE PEACE PROCESS THIS REGION HAS EVER SEEN.
AT LEAST CATCHING IT AT INCUBATION STAGE SHOULD MAKE IT EASIER TO KILL THE BLASTED THING.
TO BE HONEST, I THOUGHT WE WERE SABOTAGING A TECH-WEAPON HERE, DOCTOR. I DON'T THINK ANY OF US EXPECTED THE TARGET TO HAVE A PULSE.
THIS BEAST HAS TWENTY-TWO HEARTS AND NO RECOGNIZABLE BRAINWAVES, CYCLOPS. IT'S JUST A MELTING POT OF GENES, AND NO MORE HUMAN THAN YOU ARE, MY FRIEND --
NOW HURRY UP AND PULL THE PLUG BEFORE BASE SECURITY FIGURES OUT WHERE YOU'RE HIDING, BOY!
CYCLOPS! VORSICHT!*
*CYCLOPS! LOOK OUT!

WHAT?

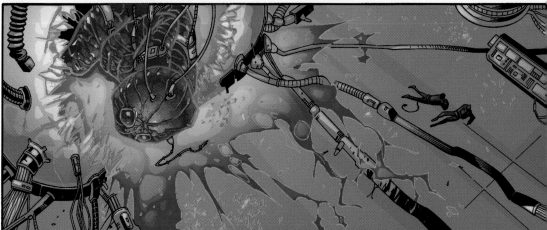

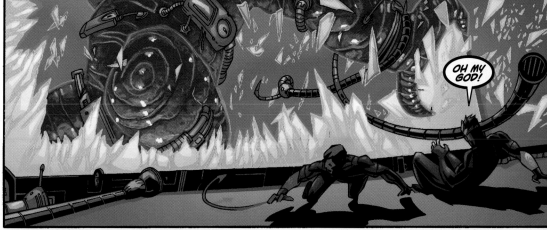

OH MY GOD!

WHAT ARE YOU WAITING FOR, NIGHTCRAWLER? GET US OUT OF HERE, MAN!

*HIT THE DETONATOR, YOU IDIOT! HIT IT!

DRUEK AUF DEN ASLOESER! DRUEK ES!*

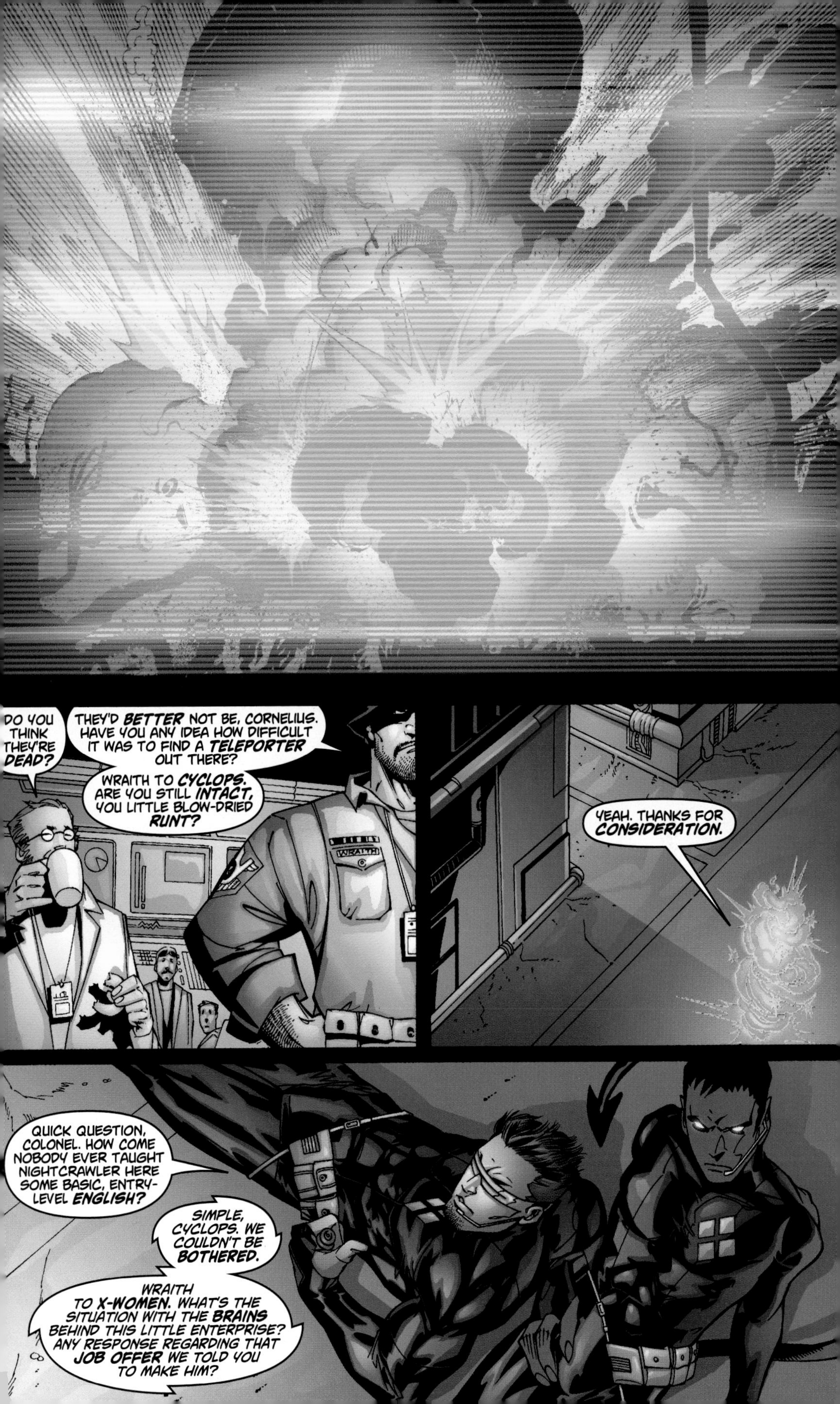
DO YOU THINK THEY'RE DEAD?
THEY'D BETTER NOT BE, CORNELIUS. HAVE YOU ANY IDEA HOW DIFFICULT IT WAS TO FIND A TELEPORTER OUT THERE?
WRAITH TO CYCLOPS. ARE YOU STILL INTACT, YOU LITTLE BLOW-DRIED RUNT?
WRAITH
YEAH. THANKS FOR CONSIDERATION.
QUICK QUESTION, COLONEL. HOW COME NOBODY EVER TAUGHT NIGHTCRAWLER HERE SOME BASIC, ENTRY-LEVEL ENGLISH?
SIMPLE, CYCLOPS. WE COULDN'T BE BOTHERED.
WRAITH TO X-WOMEN. WHAT'S THE SITUATION WITH THE BRAINS BEHIND THIS LITTLE ENTERPRISE? ANY RESPONSE REGARDING THAT JOB OFFER WE TOLD YOU TO MAKE HIM?

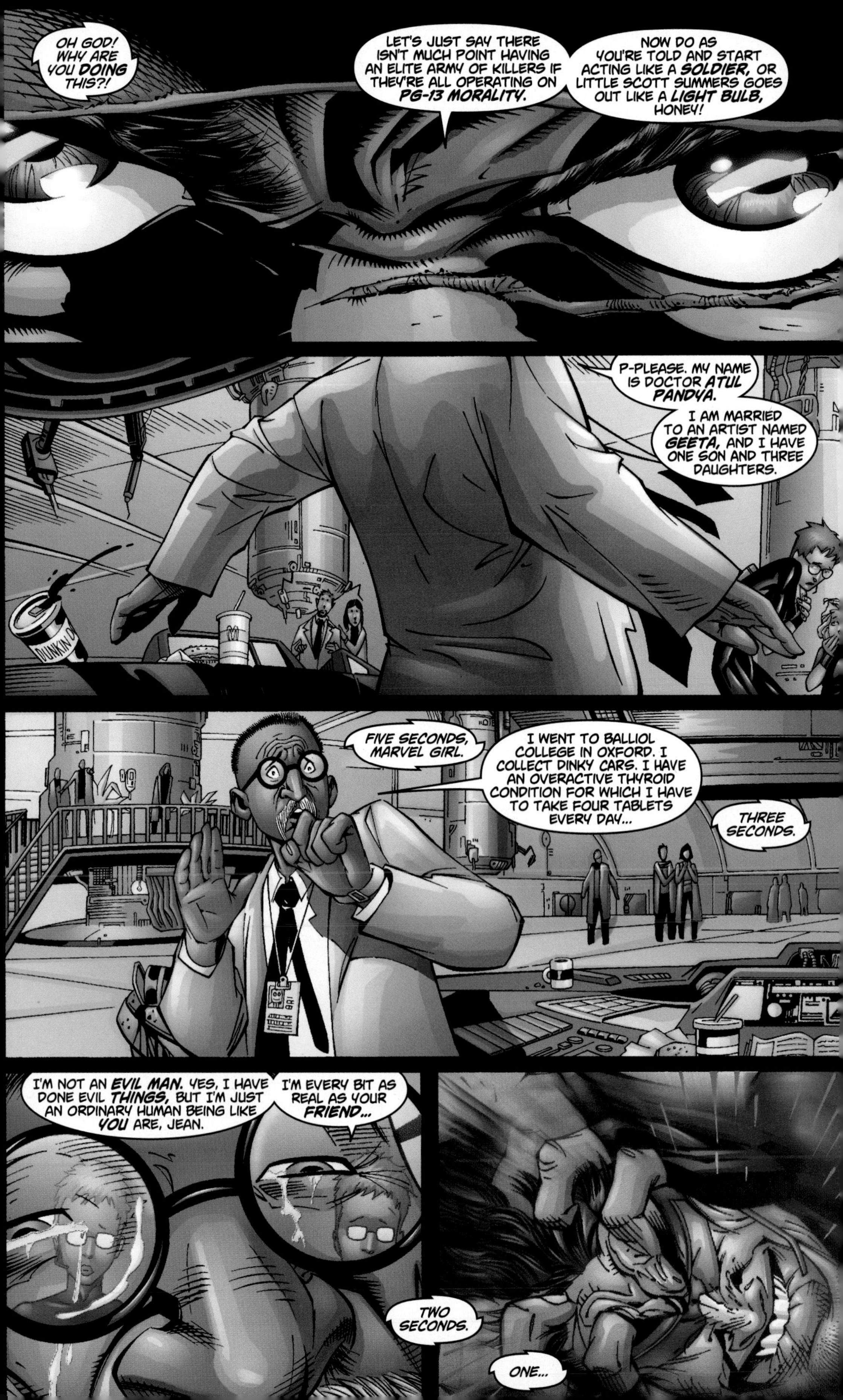
OH GOD! WHY ARE YOU DOING THIS?!
LET'S JUST SAY THERE ISN'T MUCH POINT HAVING AN ELITE ARMY OF KILLERS IF THEY'RE ALL OPERATING ON PG-13 MORALITY.
NOW DO AS YOU'RE TOLD AND START ACTING LIKE A SOLDIER, OR LITTLE SCOTT SUMMERS GOES OUT LIKE A LIGHT BULB, HONEY!
P-PLEASE. MY NAME IS DOCTOR ATUL PANDYA.
I AM MARRIED TO AN ARTIST NAMED GEETA, AND I HAVE ONE SON AND THREE DAUGHTERS.
FIVE SECONDS, MARVEL GIRL.
I WENT TO BALLIOL COLLEGE IN OXFORD. I COLLECT DINKY CARS. I HAVE AN OVERACTIVE THYROID CONDITION FOR WHICH I HAVE TO TAKE FOUR TABLETS EVERY DAY...
THREE SECONDS.
I'M NOT AN EVIL MAN. YES, I HAVE DONE EVIL THINGS, BUT I'M JUST AN ORDINARY HUMAN BEING LIKE YOU ARE, JEAN.
I'M EVERY BIT AS REAL AS YOUR FRIEND...
TWO SECONDS.
ONE...

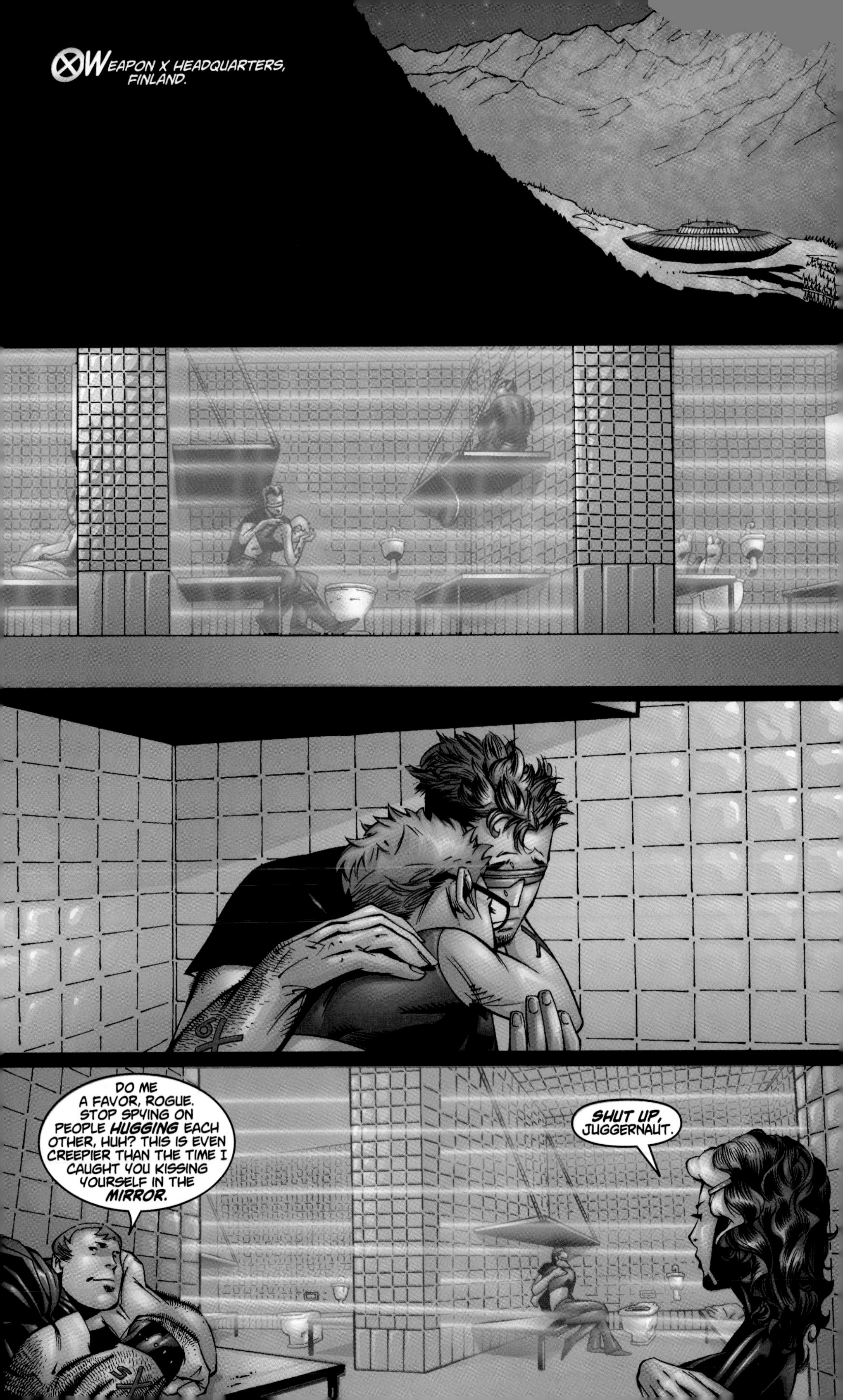
WEAPON X HEADQUARTERS, FINLAND.
DO ME A FAVOR, ROGUE. STOP SPYING ON PEOPLE HUGGING EACH OTHER, HUH? THIS IS EVEN CREEPIER THAN THE TIME I CAUGHT YOU KISSING YOURSELF IN THE MIRROR.
SHUT UP, JUGGERNAUT.

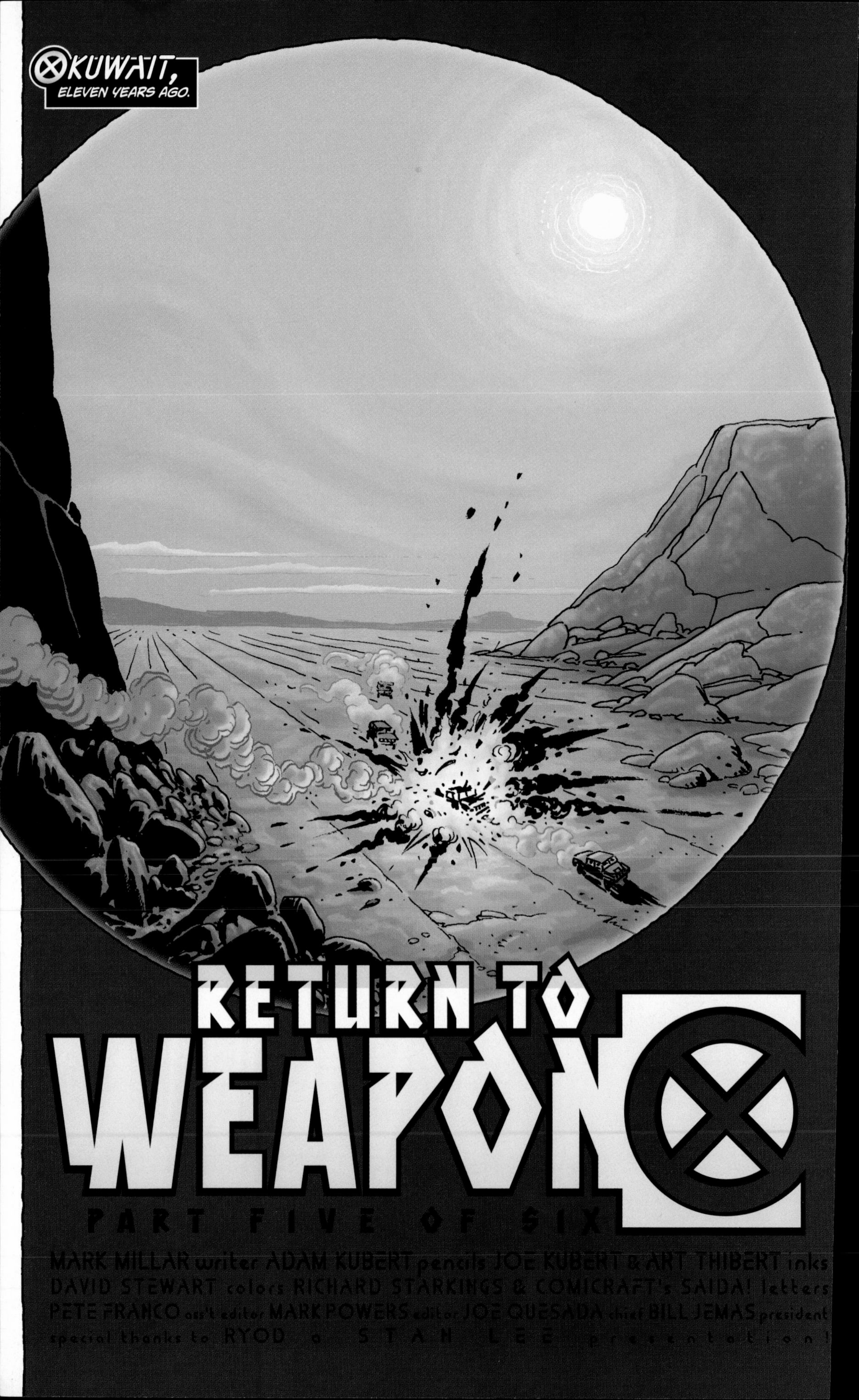
KUWAIT, ELEVEN YEARS AGO.
RETURN TO WEAPON X
PART FIVE OF SIX
MARK MILLAR writer ADAM KUBERT pencils JOE KUBERT & ART THIBERT inks
DAVID STEWART colors RICHARD STARKINGS & COMICRAFT's SAIDA! letters
PETE FRANCO ass't editor MARK POWERS editor JOE QUESADA chief BILL JEMAS president
special thanks to RYOD a STAN LEE presentation!

FIVE SIERRA FOXTROT GOLF, THIS IS NOVEMBER FOXTROT WITH OSCAR DELTA ALPHA FIVE SEVENTY-ONE! WE'RE SURROUNDED BY AN ESTIMATED TEN TO FIFTEEN *LOCALS* FIVE HUNDRED MILES SOUTH OF *AL BASRAN!*

GROUND AND AIR COVER *REQUIRED,* SIR! I REPEAT, GROUND AND AIR COVER *REQUIRED!* OVER!

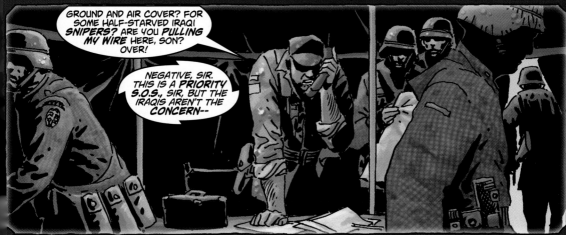

GROUND AND AIR COVER? FOR SOME HALF-STARVED IRAQI *SNIPERS?* ARE YOU *PULLING MY WIRE* HERE, SON? OVER!

NEGATIVE, SIR. THIS IS A *PRIORITY S.O.S.,* SIR, BUT THE IRAQIS AREN'T THE *CONCERN--*

THESE *IDIOTS* JUST SHELLED THE *ADAMANTIUM CAGE* WE WERE CARRYING *WEAPON X* IN! OVER!

WHAT?

YOUJAD SHAY' GHAYR MA'QOUL. IMSIK BAROUDATAK. A'TAQID ANNA WAHID MIN HALAMIRKAN LA YAZAL HAYYAN. *

*THERE IS SOMETHING **WRONG** HERE. GRAB YOUR RIFLES. I THINK ONE OF THE **AMERICANS** IS STILL **ALIVE** OUT THERE.

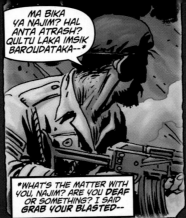

MA BIKA YA NAJIM? HAL ANTA ATRASH? QULTU LAKA IMSIK BAROUDATAKA--*

*WHAT'S THE MATTER WITH YOU, NAJIM? ARE YOU **DEAF** OR SOMETHING? I SAID **GRAB YOUR BLASTED--**

IBIN ALQAHBA?*

*CENSORED.

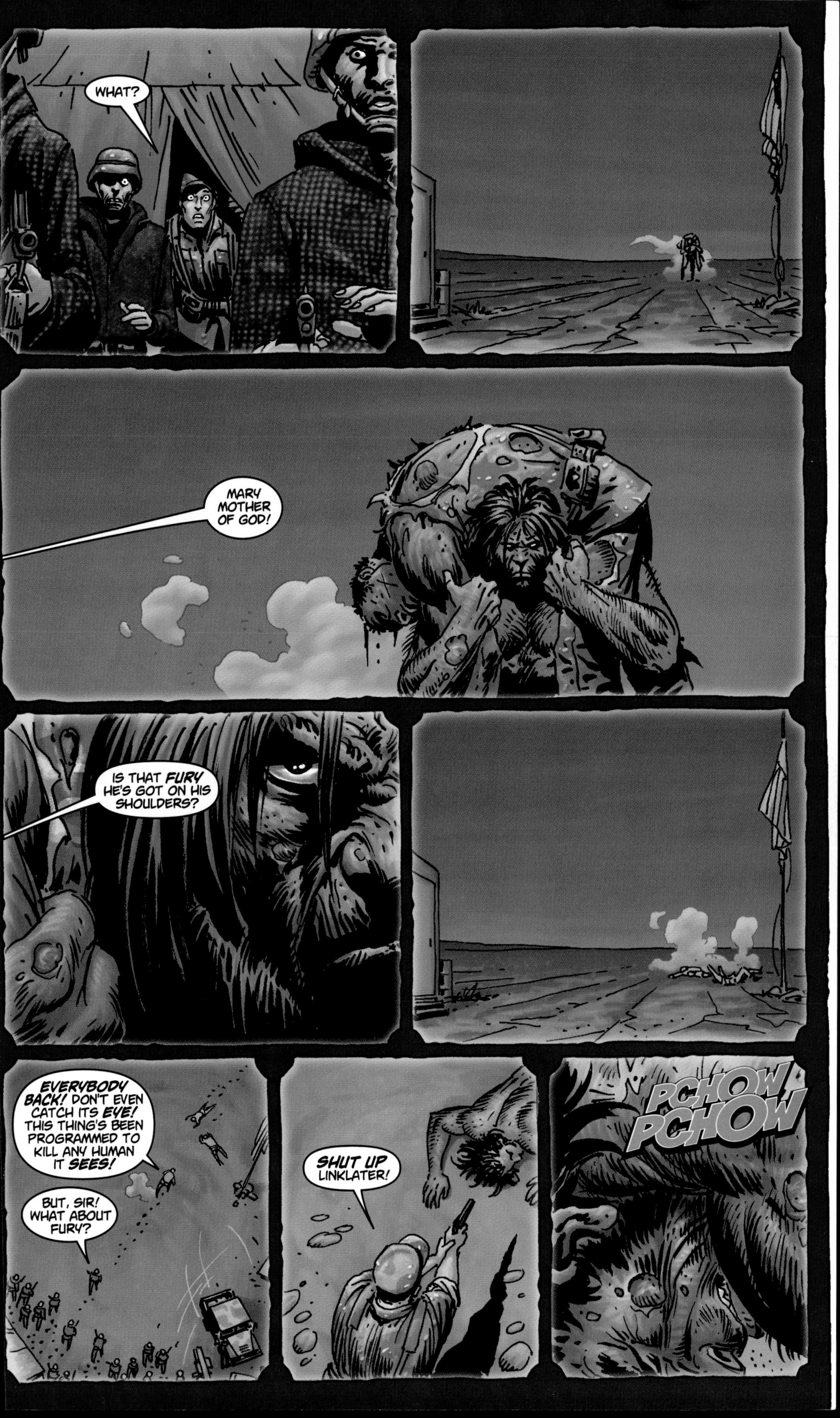
WHAT?
MARY MOTHER OF GOD!
IS THAT FURY HE'S GOT ON HIS SHOULDERS?
EVERYBODY BACK! DON'T EVEN CATCH ITS EYE! THIS THING'S BEEN PROGRAMMED TO KILL ANY HUMAN IT SEES!
BUT, SIR! WHAT ABOUT FURY?
SHUT UP LINKLATER!
PCHOW PCHOW

ARE YOU AWAKE, WOLVERINE?

I HOPE SO, BECAUSE THERE'S SOMETHING I REALLY WANT TO TELL YOU BEFORE THE DOCTORS TAKE A SCRUBBING BRUSH TO OUR MEMORIES.

I WANT YOU TO KNOW THAT I FINALLY *UNDERSTAND.*

AFTER SIX WEEKS IN THIS HORRIBLE PLACE, I THINK I KNOW WHY YOU HATED PEOPLE AS MUCH AS YOU *DID* AND I WANT TO APOLOGIZE FOR *JUDGING* YOU BACK IN *WASHINGTON.*

THE FACT THAT YOU COULD STILL EMBRACE THE PROFESSOR'S DREAM AFTER ALL THOSE YEARS OF BEING *TORTURED* IN HERE AND THE FACT THAT YOU CAME *BACK* TO THIS HELLHOLE JUST TO *SAVE* US...

...WELL, I GUESS YOU MUST HAVE MORE *HOPE* IN YOUR HEART THAN JUST ABOUT ANYONE I'VE EVER MET. AND I'M REALLY, REALLY SORRY FOR DOUBTING YOUR *SINCERITY.*

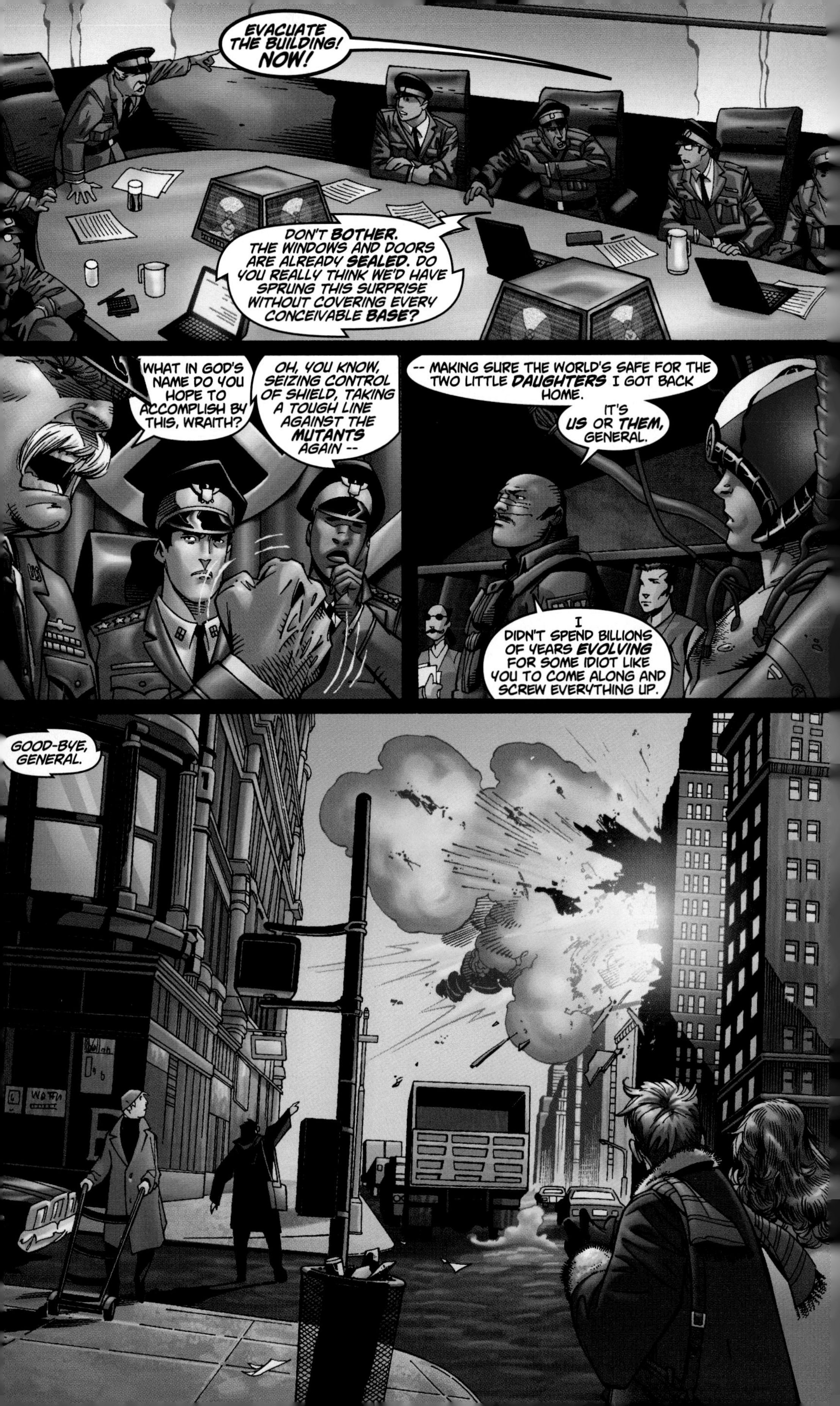
EVACUATE THE BUILDING! NOW!
DON'T BOTHER. THE WINDOWS AND DOORS ARE ALREADY SEALED. DO YOU REALLY THINK WE'D HAVE SPRUNG THIS SURPRISE WITHOUT COVERING EVERY CONCEIVABLE BASE?
WHAT IN GOD'S NAME DO YOU HOPE TO ACCOMPLISH BY THIS, WRAITH?
OH, YOU KNOW, SEIZING CONTROL OF SHIELD, TAKING A TOUGH LINE AGAINST THE MUTANTS AGAIN --
-- MAKING SURE THE WORLD'S SAFE FOR THE TWO LITTLE DAUGHTERS I GOT BACK HOME.
IT'S US OR THEM, GENERAL.
I DIDN'T SPEND BILLIONS OF YEARS EVOLVING FOR SOME IDIOT LIKE YOU TO COME ALONG AND SCREW EVERYTHING UP.
GOOD-BYE, GENERAL.

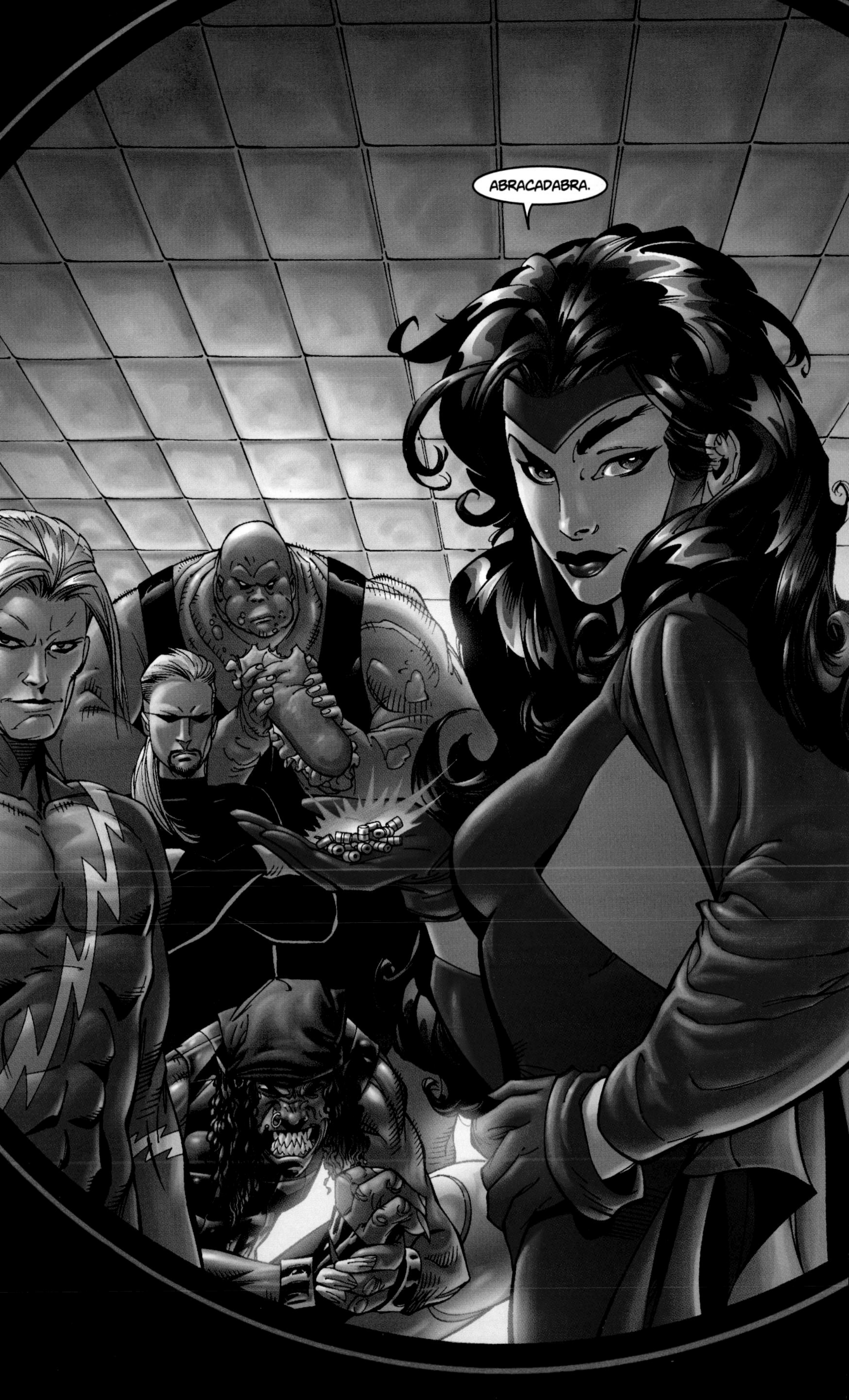
ABRACADABRA.

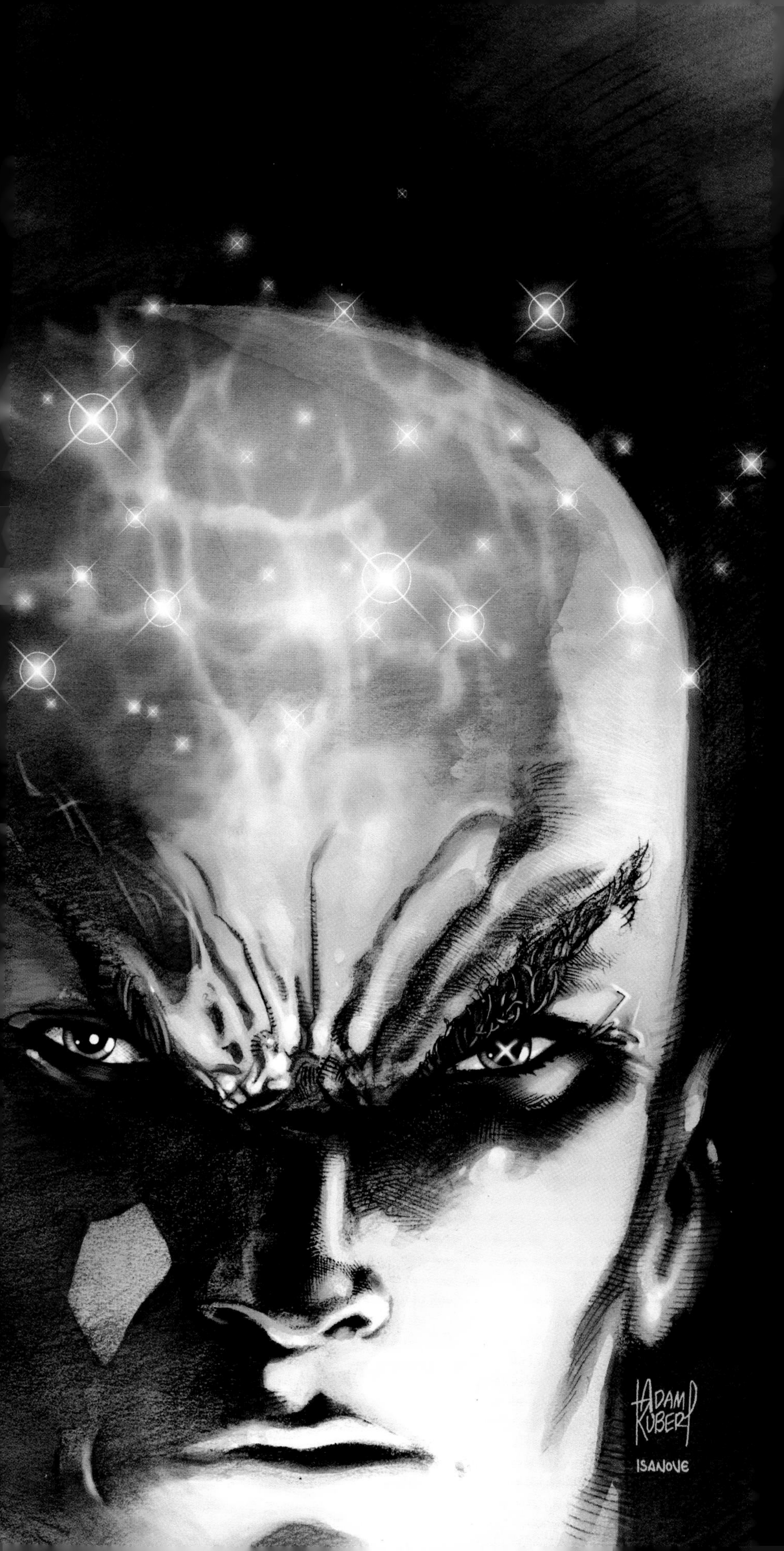
ADAM KUBERT
ISANOVE

ICEMAN.

STORM.

SCARLET WITCH.

NIGHTCRAWLER.

COLOSSUS.

TOAD.

BEAST.

CYCLOPS.

QUICKSILVER.

THE POWER'S DOWN IN HOLDING BLOCK THREE! HIT THE BACKUP GENERATORS!

DON'T WASTE YOUR *BREATH*, LITTLE MAN. THE *BLOB'S* ALREADY *EATEN* THEM.

OH DEAR GOD! THE MUTANTS HAVE TAKEN OVER HALF THE BLASTED *COMPOUND*, CORNELIUS!

CAN'T YOU DO SOMETHING CLEVER WITH XAVIER'S *PSYCHIC ABILITIES* AND GIVE THEM ALL *ANEURYSMS* OR SOMETHING?

NOT WHILE THE *ELECTRICITY* IS DOWN, COLONEL WRAITH. IN FACT, NOW THAT THERE'S NOTHING KEEPING HIM IN *CHECK*, OUR BIGGEST CONCERN SHOULD BE WHAT XAVIER'S GOING TO DO WHEN HE *WAKES UP.*

WHAT?

FREEZE, YOU FREAKS!

YOU KNOW, YOU REALLY SHOULDN'T GIVE ICEMAN OPENINGS LIKE THAT, MISTER.

WHAT MAKES YOU THINK HE'S GONNA WAKE UP?

WELL, WHY SHOULDN'T HE? THE ONLY THING THAT WAS LETTING US CONTROL HIM WERE THE NEURAL CLAMPS, AND NOW THAT THE MACHINE ISN'T WORKING...

...WELL, MY GUESS IS WE'VE GOT APPROXIMATELY FIVE TO TEN MINUTES TO GET OUT OF HERE.

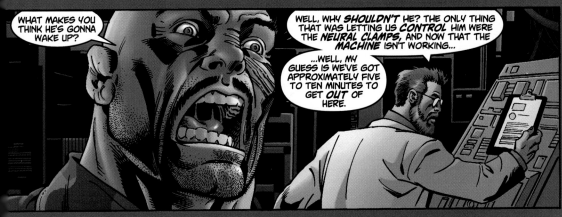

UNACCEPTABLE, CORNELIUS. ABSOLUTELY OFF-THE-SCALE UNACCEPTABLE...

WRAITH! WHAT ON EARTH ARE YOU DOING?

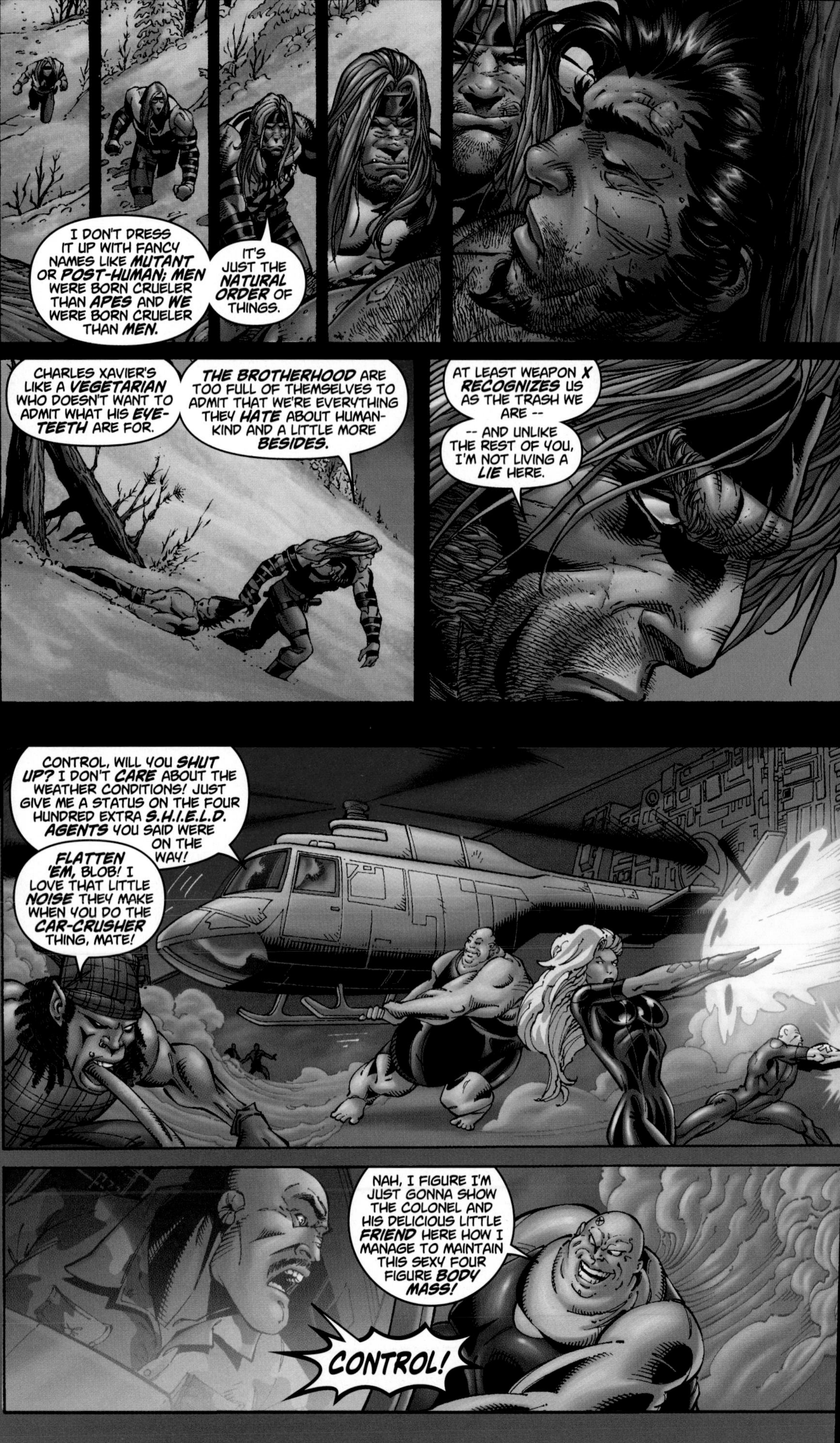
I DON'T DRESS IT UP WITH FANCY NAMES LIKE MUTANT OR POST-HUMAN; MEN WERE BORN CRUELER THAN APES AND WE WERE BORN CRUELER THAN MEN.
IT'S JUST THE NATURAL ORDER OF THINGS.
CHARLES XAVIER'S LIKE A VEGETARIAN WHO DOESN'T WANT TO ADMIT WHAT HIS EYE-TEETH ARE FOR.
THE BROTHERHOOD ARE TOO FULL OF THEMSELVES TO ADMIT THAT WE'RE EVERYTHING THEY HATE ABOUT HUMAN-KIND AND A LITTLE MORE BESIDES.
AT LEAST WEAPON X RECOGNIZES US AS THE TRASH WE ARE --
-- AND UNLIKE THE REST OF YOU, I'M NOT LIVING A LIE HERE.
CONTROL, WILL YOU SHUT UP? I DON'T CARE ABOUT THE WEATHER CONDITIONS! JUST GIVE ME A STATUS ON THE FOUR HUNDRED EXTRA S.H.I.E.L.D. AGENTS YOU SAID WERE ON THE WAY!
FLATTEN 'EM, BLOB! I LOVE THAT LITTLE NOISE THEY MAKE WHEN YOU DO THE CAR-CRUSHER THING, MATE!
NAH, I FIGURE I'M JUST GONNA SHOW THE COLONEL AND HIS DELICIOUS LITTLE FRIEND HERE HOW I MANAGE TO MAINTAIN THIS SEXY FOUR FIGURE BODY MASS!
CONTROL!

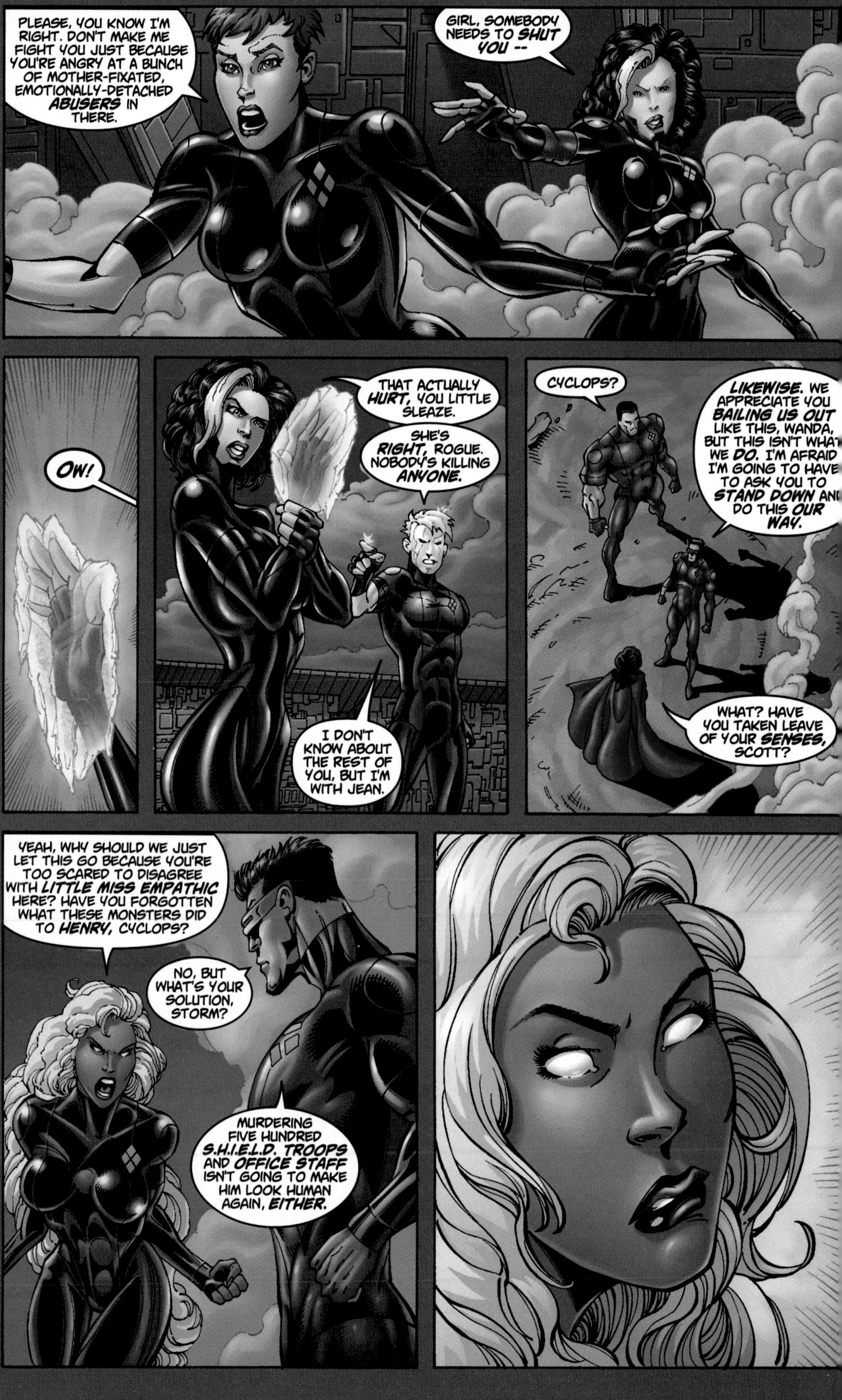
PLEASE, YOU KNOW I'M RIGHT. DON'T MAKE ME FIGHT YOU JUST BECAUSE YOU'RE ANGRY AT A BUNCH OF MOTHER-FIXATED, EMOTIONALLY-DETACHED ABUSERS IN THERE.
GIRL, SOMEBODY NEEDS TO SHUT YOU --
OW!
THAT ACTUALLY HURT, YOU LITTLE SLEAZE.
SHE'S RIGHT, ROGUE. NOBODY'S KILLING ANYONE.
I DON'T KNOW ABOUT THE REST OF YOU, BUT I'M WITH JEAN.
CYCLOPS?
LIKEWISE. WE APPRECIATE YOU BAILING US OUT LIKE THIS, WANDA, BUT THIS ISN'T WHAT WE DO. I'M AFRAID I'M GOING TO HAVE TO ASK YOU TO STAND DOWN AND DO THIS OUR WAY.
WHAT? HAVE YOU TAKEN LEAVE OF YOUR SENSES, SCOTT?
YEAH, WHY SHOULD WE JUST LET THIS GO BECAUSE YOU'RE TOO SCARED TO DISAGREE WITH LITTLE MISS EMPATHIC HERE? HAVE YOU FORGOTTEN WHAT THESE MONSTERS DID TO HENRY, CYCLOPS?
NO, BUT WHAT'S YOUR SOLUTION, STORM?
MURDERING FIVE HUNDRED S.H.I.E.L.D. TROOPS AND OFFICE STAFF ISN'T GOING TO MAKE HIM LOOK HUMAN AGAIN, EITHER.

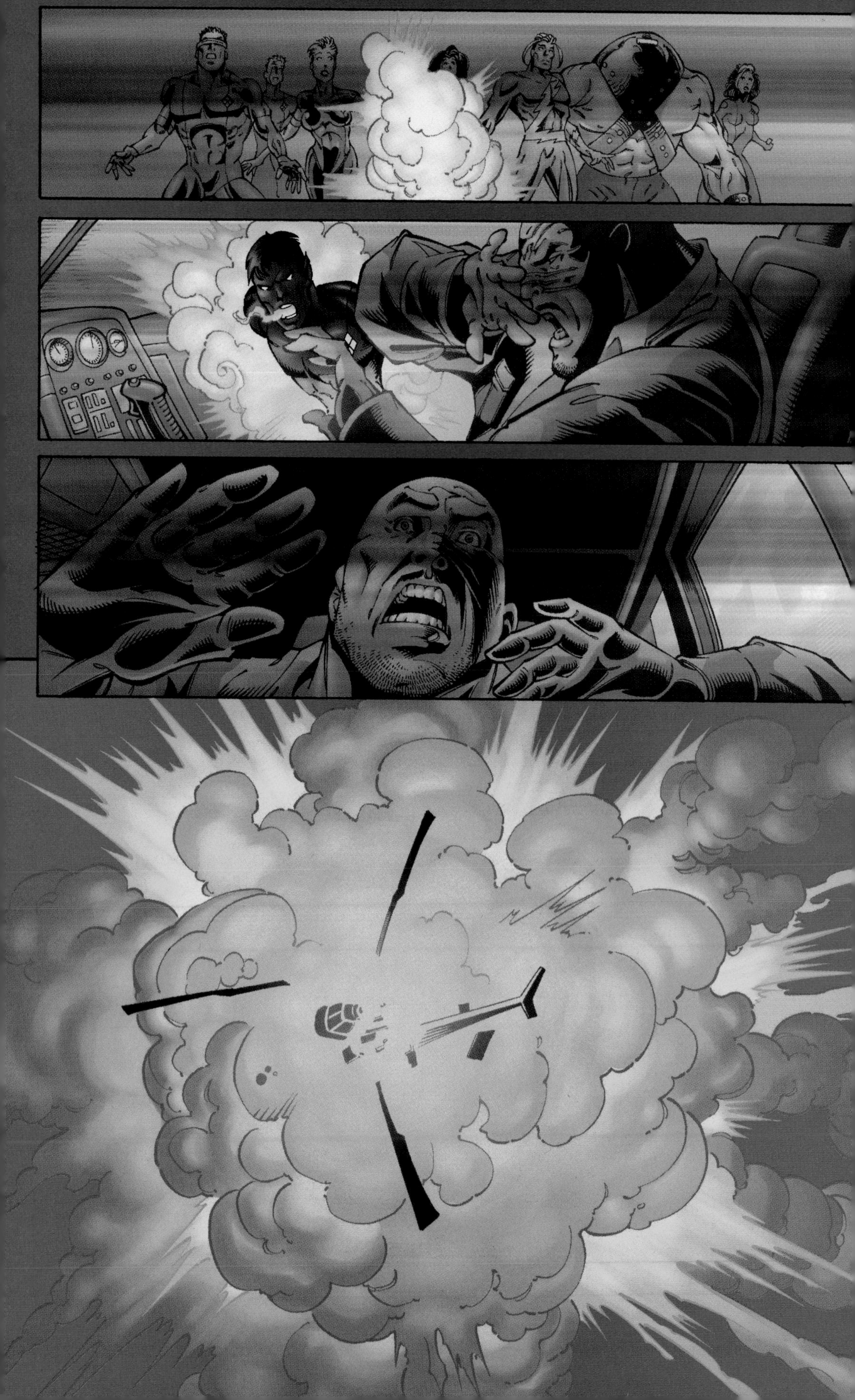

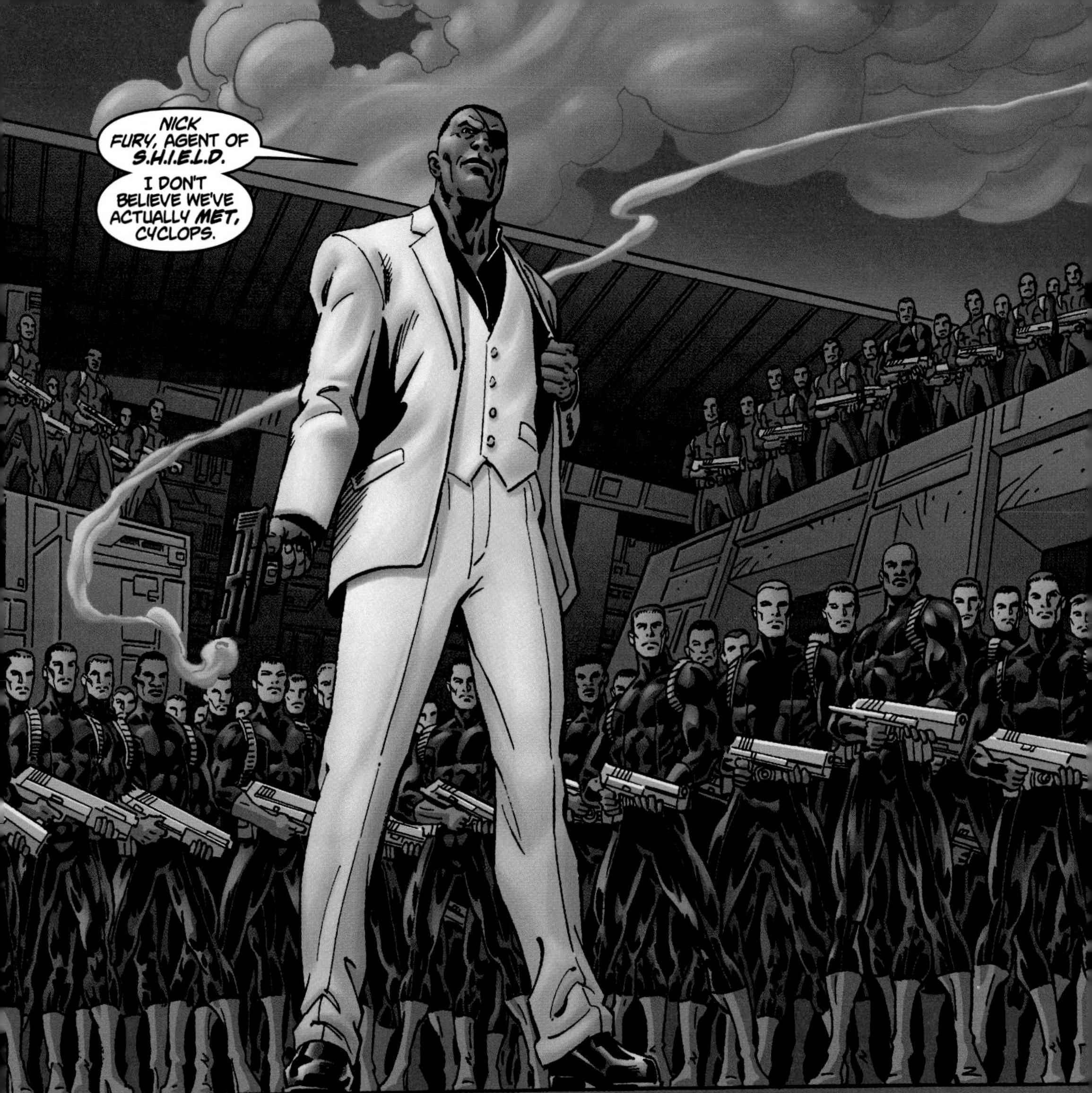
NICK FURY, AGENT OF S.H.I.E.L.D.
I DON'T BELIEVE WE'VE ACTUALLY MET, CYCLOPS.

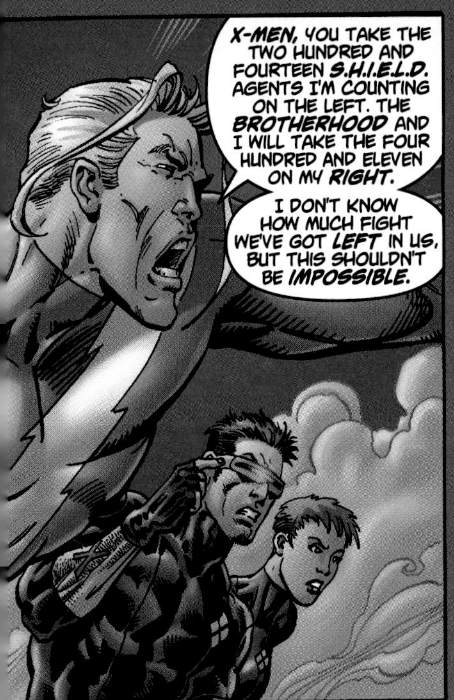
X-MEN, YOU TAKE THE TWO HUNDRED AND FOURTEEN S.H.I.E.L.D. AGENTS I'M COUNTING ON THE LEFT. THE BROTHERHOOD AND I WILL TAKE THE FOUR HUNDRED AND ELEVEN ON MY RIGHT.
I DON'T KNOW HOW MUCH FIGHT WE'VE GOT LEFT IN US, BUT THIS SHOULDN'T BE IMPOSSIBLE.

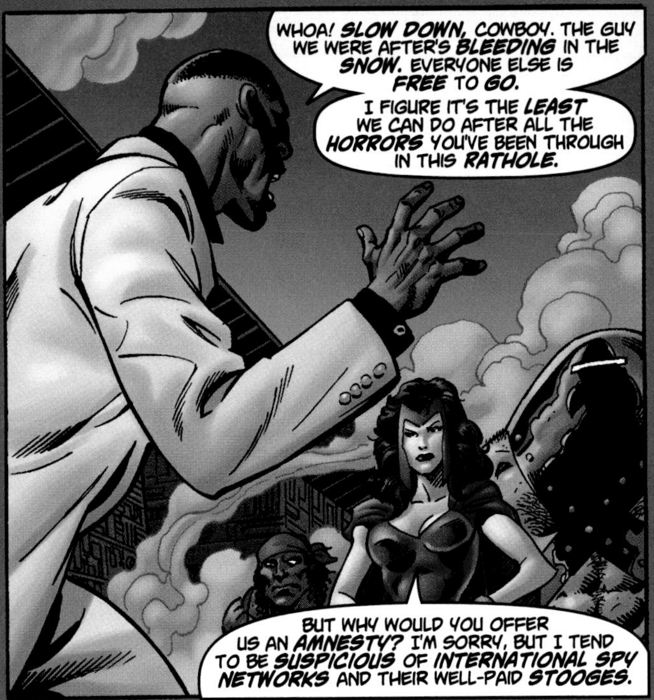
WHOA! SLOW DOWN, COWBOY. THE GUY WE WERE AFTER'S BLEEDING IN THE SNOW. EVERYONE ELSE IS FREE TO GO.
I FIGURE IT'S THE LEAST WE CAN DO AFTER ALL THE HORRORS YOU'VE BEEN THROUGH IN THIS RATHOLE.
BUT WHY WOULD YOU OFFER US AN AMNESTY? I'M SORRY, BUT I TEND TO BE SUSPICIOUS OF INTERNATIONAL SPY NETWORKS AND THEIR WELL-PAID STOOGES.

I KNOW I PROMISED HANK I'D GET SOME SLEEP, BUT I JUST WANTED TO SAY HOW VERY *PROUD* I AM OF YOU, JEAN.

THE ENTIRE CLASS DID WELL, OF COURSE, BUT THE WAY YOU AND BEAST CONDUCTED YOURSELVES IN MY ABSENCE WAS *EXCEPTIONAL*.

WE'RE SUPPOSED TO BE A *CATALYST* BETWEEN THESE TWO *WARRING SPECIES*. THE MOMENT WE RESORT TO *MURDER*, I'M AFRAID OUR CREDIBILITY DISAPPEARS *FOREVER*.

DON'T TELL *WOLVERINE*, PROFESSOR. HE'LL BE ON THE FIRST BUS BACK TO *CANADA*.

I HOPE YOU WERE *SMILING* WHEN YOU SAID THAT, MISS GREY?